OLD WEST

Adventures in Arizona

by

Charles D. Lauer

GOLDEN
WEST ☼
PUBLISHERS

Front cover artwork by Frederic Remington

Also by Charles D. Lauer:
Tales of Arizona Territory

Library of Congress Cataloging-in-Publication Data

Lauer, Charles D.

Old West Adventures in Arizona / by Charles D. Lauer.
Bibliography
Includes index.
1. Historic sites—Arizona   2. Arizona—History, Local.
3. Frontier and pioneer life—Arizona.   I. Title.
F812.L38 1989   979.1—dc19   88-24676 CIP
ISBN 0-914846-39-6

Printed in the United States of America

2nd Printing © 1998

Information in this book is deemed to be authentic and accurate by author and publisher. However, they disclaim any liability incurred in connection with the use of information appearing in this book.

Golden West Publishers, Inc.
4113 N. Longview Ave.
Phoenix, AZ 85014, USA
(602) 265-4392

Dedication

To my wife, Mary Ruth,
and the other four-wheeling vagabonds,
Dan and Joanna Murphy,
and Weldon and Carol Minchew.

Acknowledgment

Most of the material in this volume came from the files of the Arizona Historical Society in Tucson and Phoenix, the Arizona Historical Foundation and Arizona Collection in the Hayden Library, Arizona State University, Tempe, and the Sharlot Hall Museum Research Library, Prescott.

Arizona Historical Society, Tucson: Reminiscences of Wm. M. Breakenridge, Frank C. Brophy, Mattie Sanderson Chambers, John F. Crampton, William H. Fourr, Charles O. Harrison, Emerson O. Stratton. Interviews with Wm. M. Breakenridge as told to Charles Morgan Wood and Mrs. George Kitt. Materials in reference files of M. B. Duffield and Henry Morgan. "Holbrook," master's thesis by Harold Wayte. Microfilmed files of *Arizona Daily Star* and *Tucson Citizen.* Pictures, clippings and maps from library's files.

Arizona Historical Society, Phoenix: Reminiscences of James M. Barney.

Arizona Historical Foundation and Arizona Collection, Hayden Library, Arizona State University, Tempe: Reminiscences of Madison R. Loring. Material in reference files of William S. Bichard, Frederick Brunckow, Henry Morgan. Sketch of life of M. B. Duffield by B. Sacks.

Sharlot Hall Museum Research Library, Prescott: Material in reference files of Fort Misery and John B. Howard. Genung Letter in Document File. *Plateau* Magazine, Spring 1964. Pictures and clippings from the library's files.

Newspaper sources credited in text. Pictures not otherwise credited are by the author.

Contents

PREFACE

In Arizona Territory there were places where pioneers settled or gathered that became prominent and well-known among the early settlers and travelers, but which later, because of changing circumstances, became obscure or fell into oblivion.

Such a place might have been a river bank near a rocky ford that made an easy place to cross, where someone built a wayside station to serve meals and provide lodgings for passing travelers. It might have been on a stagecoach or wagon train route, where the stagecoach company built a station to accommodate travelers or changing teams. Often, especially in desert areas, it was where that most precious of commodities, water, might be found naturally and abundantly. It might have been a mining camp, a ranch headquarters, a stockade or fort affording protection from marauding Indians.

To western historians and lovers of the Old West, these abandoned places are deeply fascinating. Where there was only virgin wilderness, where there was no touch of the hand of man, some hardy forebear made an outpost of civilization in a new land. We want to know who they were, why they came, what their life was like, why they left. What people of history, famous or notorious, prominent or obscure, may have dwelled there or passed by? Even in these late days we yearn to reach out and touch it, see it, be a part of it ourselves.

Their place names are touched with romance—camp, well, pass, spring, flat, station—from the nation's western heritage in which Americans still have a deep interest. There are no more of them; words like subdivision, condominium, apartment and suburb can never replace them. To answer our longing questions about these obscure places is, as a rule, difficult. True, there are some places where events of such magnitude occurred that chapters or entire volumes of history books have been devoted to them, such as at Apache Pass or Oatman Flat, but they are exceptions. Ghost towns are easier to document because of official records or newspaper files that have been preserved. This book has avoided towns, with one exception, because there have been so many excellent publications about them. For other places, with no official record, occasional references in old manuscripts, letters and books, and scraps of information from old newspaper files are the only sources from which insight may be gleaned.

To read them is to rediscover a past of which many have never heard. This is due in part to the cooling of old passions and the healing of old wounds, the dimming of the memory of how it was by the passage of time. There are even some in today's world that would remold history, pretend that some events never happened or that some of those who took part in them, red or white, need apologists or a new "image." They would eliminate reality from movie or television "westerns," or prevent from being shown those which these shadowy censors consider to be preserving "stereotypes." Nothing they can say or do can change the truth, however.

The Apache Indian was raised from birth in a tradition of savagery which included raiding and killing people of other tribes, and later Mexicans and Americans, as a way of life. Their method of warfare was not, except for rare occasions, pitched battles between large forces of Indians on one side and troops of soldiers on the other. Their usual warfare was murder from ambush, for which a solitary rider or miner had no warning until struck down by an arrow or bullet, or by waylaying small groups such as a wagon train or family of ranchers by striking suddenly in overwhelming numbers. They put captives to death by unspeakable tortures, or carried women and children off into slavery.

A hatred almost as bitter as that toward the Apaches existed between the Mexicans and Americans. This had its roots in the "no quarter" war for the independence of Texas from Mexico. The annexation of Texas by the United States, the war with Mexico, resentments over the Gadsden Purchase, and the migration of hordes of Texans to Arizona contributed to this flaming hatred between Americans and Mexicans in the territory. The Mexican epithet "gringo" for Americans and the American "greaser" for Mexicans were mild. Lone Mexican bandits or groups of "bandidos" raided into Arizona Territory, robbing and murdering, and escaped to sanctuary in Old Mexico. American expeditions of mercenaries sacked entire Mexican towns, or attempted to seize large parcels of Mexico to establish new states or nations.

Among Americans themselves in Arizona there was from the beginning bitter factional strife. Much of it began with the Civil

War, which ended in 1865, the year that marked the real beginning of the settlement of Arizona Territory. Northern partisans and Southern sympathizers cordially despised each other, and did not hesitate to put their loathing into action as well as words. Displaced Southerners crowded into the new territory and established a Democratic political dominance that was galling and overbearing toward their opponents. There were feuds between cattle ranchers and rustler bands of outlaws, and between cattlemen and sheepmen. There were recriminations between the settlers and the military that was there to protect them. The settlers complained that soldiers sometimes gave the Indians plenty of notice before riding out to attack them. It is important to understand these undercurrents of hatred and resentment. They constantly resurface in records of early Arizona examined by the researchers.

In library files, reference materials abound where research into these early times may be carried on. Articles and books about the West, some of them written by the pioneers themselves, are available. So are interviews with the pioneers while they still lived, preserved by able writers. Files of newspaper clippings and the old newspapers themselves on microfilm are there to be examined. In the research library of the Arizona Historical Society in Tucson and Phoenix, are manuscripts with the reminiscences of the pioneers written while they lived, many of them in their own longhand, in pencil, some on blue-lined tablet paper. Similar records, invaluable and irreplaceable, are found in the Arizona Historical Foundation and the Arizona Collection in the Hayden Library at Arizona State University in Tempe, and in the research library of the Sharlot Hall Museum in Prescott. There are still other files in historical societies and local libraries around the state.

The author wishes to express his thanks and deep appreciation to the institutions and staffs of the Arizona Historical Society in Tucson and Phoenix, the Arizona Collection and Arizona Historical Foundation, Hayden Library at Arizona State University in Tempe, Sharlot Hall Museum and Library in Prescott, Pinal County Historical Society, and the public libraries in Phoenix, Mesa and Holbrook for their assistance. No request for aid was ever too small to enlist the immediate and undivided attention of the staff person contacted. Each person did his or her utmost, to the smallest detail. Without their help this volume would never have been possible.

CHAPTER 1
The Butterfield Overland Trail

The mere mention of the name "Butterfield Overland Trail" instantly transports us to America's Old West. We rise to its legends and tales of stagecoaches careening along the rough trail between wilderness outposts and desert stations, driver and shotgun guard on their high perch seat, Wells Fargo treasure box at their feet. Our minds envision gun battles with Indians or outlaws, the pellmell run of horse or mule teams, the rude stations where hardy and colorful characters changed teams, provided barely edible meals and maintained sparse accommodations. Even today it has a powerful attraction. We want to relive it, feel ourselves a part of it. In Arizona there are places where we can still find it, see it, if we only know where to look.

A few historical facts need to be stated as background. In 1857 a New York businessman, John Butterfield, obtained a government contract to carry mail overland from St. Louis, Missouri, to San Francisco, California. "Overland" is significant since there had never been a completely successful mail route from the east to the west coast over land. Most mail had gone by sea around South America's Cape Horn, or to Panama and across the isthmus to be reloaded on ships bound for west coast ports. The same was true of passengers, except for the emigrants who had braved the elements and Indians in wagon trains over the old trails for weary months. Butterfield contracted to provide service from St. Louis to San Francisco in twenty-five days, and to begin one year after his contract date.

Consider the stupendous feat of organizing the Butterfield Overland Trail in one year. The West was a vast wilderness, much of it unknown, unexplored, unmapped. Most of the West and Southwest had been part of the United States only nine years, obtained from Mexico as a result of the war with that country. What was to become Arizona south of the Gila River had been purchased from Mexico only four years previously, because it had a flat route over which to eventually build a railroad. This was the Gadsden Purchase. Butterfield strung together trails from St. Louis southwesterly through Indian territory to El Paso, Texas, then westerly across New Mexico territory, of which Arizona was then a part, to the Colorado

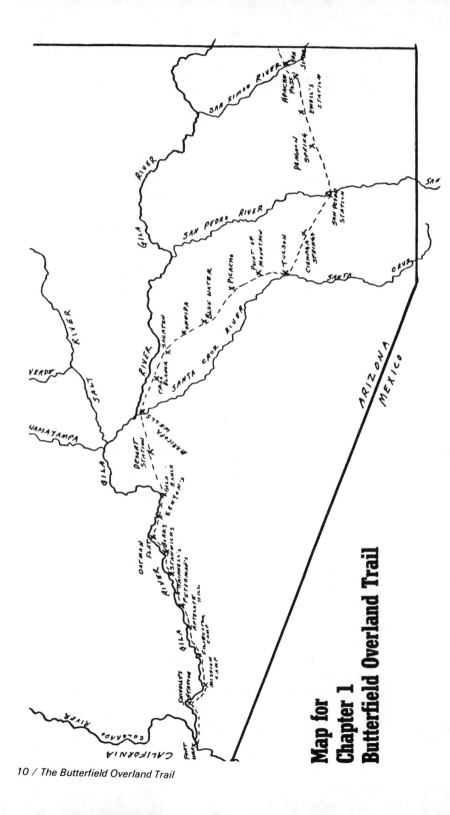

**Map for
Chapter 1
Butterfield Overland Trail**

River, and across southern California to Los Angeles and northward to San Francisco. Stagecoaches of various types were purchased, mules to be used to pull the coaches were obtained. Stations were established approximately every twenty to twenty-five miles along the more than 2,800-mile route. Most of the stations were adobe, but there were ten built of rock as fortresses against Indian attack.

The trail across what would become Arizona Territory was 437 miles. Twenty-six stations were established across the Arizona desert trail. It followed the old southern emigrant trail from waterhole to well to river, because water was the principal consideration and the reason for location of almost every station. The trail entered Arizona near Stein's Peak through Doubtful Canyon, and the first station was on the San Simon River near where the community of San Simon is today. From there it entered the famed, but dark and bloody, Apache Pass, through the Chiricahua Mountains, home of the fiercest and most warlike of all the Apache tribes, the Chiricahua Apaches. Eighteen miles from San Simon a rock station was built in the pass, a mile from Apache Spring. Another chapter will deal with the history of Apache Pass in which the station played a prominent part.

Through the pass the trail wound, and out into Sulphur Springs Valley where some fifteen miles farther Ewell's Station was established. The location was for changing teams only, and was near Ewell's Spring as a source of water. The trail then ran southwesterly toward Dragoon Spring station 25 miles away. Part of it crossed an ancient dry lake bed known as the Willcox Playa. All of this portion of the trail passed through the heart of Apache country, as the Dragoon Spring station was on the north slope of the Dragoon Mountains, in which was the stronghold of the great Chiricahua Apache chief, Cochise. Butterfield's agents were able to make terms with Cochise to allow stagecoaches to pass unmolested, as the chief was at that time at peace with the Americans. After an incident in 1861 that caused Cochise to take to the warpath, no Butterfield stagecoach was ever safe from attack again.

A half-mile from Dragoon Spring the last of the rock stations was built in Dragoon Pass. A subsequent chapter will give more of the bloody history of this station. Remains of it are still to be found today, preserved by the United States Forest Service. To the visitor familiar with its past, there is an air of solemn mystery about the old ruin and the graveyard in its solitary isolation. West of Dragoon Spring 21 miles was the next of the stations, the San Pedro River station on the banks of that stream. The Butterfield company built a bridge across the river here, but the bridge was washed away in a flood in 1883, more than 20 years after the line had ceased to operate. The station was across the river from the present town of Benson.

West of the San Pedro about 23 miles, the Cienega Springs station was built on the banks of Pantano Wash across from the spot where Cienega Creek enters the wash. This station also has a long and bloody history. It was used by other stage lines long after Butterfield had ceased operations, and, exposed as it was in Apache country, was many times attacked, burned and built again. In 1867, W. A. Smith and three companions were attacked at the station, and all were killed by the Apaches except Smith. He shotgunned eight of the Indians to death, and lived to be known as "Shotgun" Smith for the rest of his life. In 1870, it was known as Miller's Station when it was again attacked and destroyed by Apaches. Two men, one of them a mail carrier, were killed in this raid.

The next stop on the trail, 25 miles west of Cienega Springs, was Tucson, at that time the only settlement other than Indian villages in Arizona. It had once been the site of a Sobaipuri Indian village, and was founded when the Spanish established a presidio and outpost against the Apaches there in 1776. At the time of the operation of the Butterfield route the population was only about 150 people, but as the only settlement in the limitless wilderness, it was an important station. It was the only place in southern Arizona that was a safe haven from the Apaches, for while it had been attacked many times while under Spanish and Mexican control, it had never fallen to the Indians. With the outbreak of the Civil War and withdrawal of troops from the territory to fight in that war, the Apaches believed they had won their battle and stepped up their raids on the few remaining outpoasts. Most of these outposts were abandoned and their occupants fled to Tucson for safety.

Since there were no dependable sources of water in the vast Sonoran desert west of Tucson, the Butterfield Overland Trail followed the old emigrant trail in swinging northward to follow the Gila River the rest of the way across Arizona to the

Colorado River and California beyond. The trail followed closely the Santa Cruz River, sometimes right in the river bed itself when it was dry, for 18 miles northwest to the Point of Mountain (Pointer Mountain) Station. Its location was near the water tower at the railroad way station of Rillito. Here only teams were changed en route to the next important station, 27 miles away, at Picacho Peak.

As it was about halfway between Tucson and the Gila Rver, Picacho had long been an overnight camp location for travelers across Arizona. It was on the western fringe of Apache territory and close to the lands of the Pima, Papago and Maricopa Indians, desert tribes always friendly to the whites, and deadly enemies of the Apaches who raided them at will for their few possessions and to carry off their women and children into slavery. The Picacho station was directly across from the peak, near where there is now a freeway interchange. The station provided overnight accommodations and depended on a dug well for water.

Its situation near a familiar landmark and close to an ancient Apache war trail made the Picacho Pass station a frequent

At the site of the white building across the road is said to be the location of the Butterfield stage station in Sacaton. The monument is to Mathew B. Juan, Pima Indian, first American slain in a great battle of World War I.

target for Apache raids. Stock was often driven away, and there were stiff fights between raiding Indians and station occupants and travelers. An early Tucsonian named Charley Harrison told of one of these fights, giving the year as 1885, though that date may be approximate since his reminiscences were recorded many years later, and because in 1885 the railroad ran past the Picacho Station. Harrison recalled traveling from Montezuma, probably the Montezuma Store between Sacaton and Florence, to Tucson with a party of about 12 people. At Picacho Pass they were set upon by 30 to 40 Apaches. The fight lasted several hours, and ended when other travelers on the trail arrived and reinforced Harrison's party.

From Picacho Peak the Butterfield Trail gradually veered northward toward the Gila River and the Pima villages. Fourteen miles away and approximately three miles northeast of the highway at the present town of Eloy, the Blue Water Station was established. Nothing remains of it today; it was located in what is now a farmer's field. This old station, however, saw its share of stark tragedy and bloody death. The company sank a well that was 175 feet deep, and for a while it was the only well between the Gila River and Tucson. As such, it attracted not only travelers but Indians as well. The station was in use from the time the well was dug in 1859 until as late as 1879 at least, long after the demise of the Butterfield Route in 1861.

The reminiscences of William (Billy) Fourr, a famous Arizona pioneer who owned a cattle ranch in the Dragoon Mountains and once owned the Oatman Flat station further west on the Butterfield Route, are the source of this bloody incident at Blue Water station. In 1861, after abandonment of the station by Butterfield, the well was so important to the military and other travelers that two soldiers were always stationed there to provide the station keeper and travelers with some protection from Apaches. A Mexican family was employed to occupy the station and sell water to passersby with stock at fifteen cents per head. The station and its corrals were some 400 to 500 yards from the well, and the Apaches on the warpath made it a habit to water at the well during the night if there were no encampments about. The Mexicans and soldiers locked themselves behind the thick adobe walls of the station house to sleep at night, but in the morning there frequently were tracks of Apache raiders to be found around the well.

The soldiers had a small cannon that they had packed in on a burro. One night the soldiers loaded the cannon with scrap iron and nails, aimed it at the well, and one of the soldiers watched from the shadows of the corral in the light of a full moon. About midnight a string of mounted Apaches silently made their way to the well, and, feeling that the station occupants were sleeping and that they were safe, got down and stood around the well. As they were letting down one of the two buckets, the soldier touched off the cannon. He did not approach the well that night, but in the morning, after carefully looking around for Indians, the soldiers finally approached the well.

A few Indian ponies were standing nearby, and there were bloody pools everywhere around the well. With their rifles at the ready, the soldiers scouted the area and found two dead Apaches that had managed to crawl away for some distance. The soldiers at length went back to the well to water their stock and the Indian ponies that had been captured. Upon raising the bucket they found the water also bloody, and peering into the well found that there was a dead Indian at the bottom. This presented a problem that neither of the soldiers was anxious to solve. They had plenty of water inside the house for themselves, but they needed to water stock, and soon there would be travelers on the road who would need water for their animals. Neither soldier wanted to go down into the well, tie the dead Indian to a rope to be removed, and clean out the well.

After some thought they hit upon a plan. They hid one of the buckets and waited. Presently a group of Mexicans approached with a train of burros, and, of course, wanted to water their animals. The soldiers told them that one of the buckets was at the bottom of the well, and that if one of the group would go down after it, they could water their animals without paying. This the Mexicans were happy to do, and one of them sat down upon the other bucket and held the rope. He was lowered to the bottom, where he came upon the body, and called frantically to be raised up to the top again. The soldiers, however, now had the man at the bottom of the well where they wanted him.

The Mexican did not want to touch the dead Indian, but he had no choice. He stood on a curbing on the side of the well, and finally got up the nerve to tie the body to the bucket rope with another rope that was wrapped about his waist. The dead man was hauled up, but the Mexican's work wasn't done. He was made to stay down until he had cleaned out the bottom of the well, including the scrap iron that had been fired from the cannon and fallen in. Finally, the hood-winked man was hauled up, the other bucket was produced, his animals were watered and he was paid for his work. It was some time later that the water was considered safe for humans to drink again.

One of the principal hazards of keeping one of the remote stage stations was the ever-present possibility of being robbed. Located as they were far from banks, the station owners had to conceal their money, and frequently they were held up, tortured to make them tell where the money was hidden, then all too often killed and the station burned. Billy Fourr tells the story of the massacre of the Baker family at Blue Water Station on December 21, 1871.

John W. Baker was an industrious man who had accumulated a stake while serving as wagonmaster for a Tucson freighter. He brought his wife and small son from Illinois, and leased the Blue Water Station, where he operated a small store in addition to providing accommodations for travelers. Another child was born, the Baker family prospered, and they decided to give up the station and purchase a farm near Florence. For some time Baker had employed three Mexicans to cut wild hay for him, and when paying them off for the last time remarked that he would no longer need their services as he was going to buy a farm. This remark probably cost him his life, for the Mexicans now knew that he had a good sum of money around.

He paid them off in the presence of some white teamsters, with whom the Mexicans could have obtained transportation away from the station, but they did not leave. In the act of handing something to one of the Mexicans, Baker was shot dead with a pistol by the other two. His wife, hearing the shots, came to her husband's aid, carrying their baby. She was killed by a blast from the station's shotgun; the infant died when it fell to the floor. The four-year-old son was killed by a pistol shot through his back while running from the scene.

After murdering the Baker family, the Mexicans ransacked the house and its furnishings and trunks. What they took with them, other than the family's two horses, is unknown. The murderers fled toward Old Mexico, leaving the dead bodies where they fell. Some Mexican boys brought news of the slaughter to the Picacho Station, from where a relief party hurried, found the bodies, and buried the family in a single grave by the roadside near their desert home. Armed parties immediately began pursuit of the killers, and rewards totaling $2,100 were posted for their capture, but they escaped into Mexico and were never caught.

According to Fourr, a Mexican innocent of the murder of the Bakers lost his life at the hands of vigilantes near Phoenix because of it. The Mexican stole a cow and drove it to a butcher shop operated by another Mexican, who bought the cow and slaughtered it. The farmer who owned the animal trailed it to the butcher shop, discovered what had happened and identified the cow thief. When caught, the thief admitted stealing the cow, somewhat to clear the butcher. The vigilantes, however, noticed that the thief's wife was "wearing a fine gold ring that resembled Mrs. Baker's ring," so they hung the Mexican to a high gate post in broad daylight. Then they returned to the butcher shop to find that its terrified owner, fearing the same fate, had fled in such haste that he did not even take the money in the till with him. He also escaped into Mexico and was never seen again.

Billy Fourr also recounts the murder of two Mexican sheepherders at Blue Water Station by men he knew, but would identify only as "V. M. and the Phoenix barley sack thief." The sheepherders had finished their drive at Prescott and had been paid off by the owner of the flock. They bought some new outfits with their pay, clothes, six-shooters and good ponies, and started toward the Rio Grande country. Southward through Phoenix they went on their way to strike the Butterfield trail. As they passed through Phoenix, the "barley sack thief," a tramp white man, saw them and surmised that they were the owners of the sheep and would have a great deal more money than of course they had. The white man stole a horse and set out on the trail of the Mexicans.

As he passed travelers, the "sack thief" inquired about the sheepherders and stayed on their trail. When men in a wagon train said that the sheepherders were only a short distance ahead, the trailer claimed that the two were horse thieves whom he was following, and asked for someone to go along and help capture them. A man traveling with the train but not employed by it asked if it was certain that the Mexicans had stolen the horses, and was assured that they had. This man, whom Fourr called V. M., then agreed to accompany the "sack thief." They

Eighteen mule team and freight wagon of Matt Cavaness at Gila Ranch Station near Gila Bend, 1874. The station was owned by A. E. Decker and Thomas Childs. (Courtesy Arizona Historical Society)

traveled all night, and just after daylight found the sheepherders at Blue Water Station.

The "sack thief" told V. M. that they must shoot the Mexicans on sight, or risk being killed themselves. At this, V. M. held back, and told the "sack thief" just to call on the two men to surrender. The "sack thief" would have none of this, however. He jerked his gun and opened fire without warning, killing one of the Mexicans. The other tried to flee, but was shot out of the saddle by the two white men. The "sack thief" began going through the pockets of the murdered men, much to the displeasure of V. M. When the "sack thief" began complaining that there was little money and should have been a lot more because the sheep must have sold for at least $5,000, V. M. at last realized what had happened, and that he had been duped into becoming an accomplice to murder.

The two murderers brazenly entered Blue Water Station and ordered breakfast. While there, they quarreled in loud voices, one complaining that there was so little money on the dead men, the other that he had been decoyed into a murder plot. To the station's cook who overheard them, they told the story of shooting two Mexican horse thieves and that they were going to Tucson to report to the sheriff. The cook, however, wrote his suspicions in a note to the sheriff and gave it to the driver of the next stagecoach to deliver. Upon receiving the note, the sheriff took a posse backtracking on the trail and arrested the killers.

At his trial, the "sack thief" was convicted and sentenced to 99 years in Yuma prison. For some reason, V. M. was not tried but held in jail, and one night both men along with four or five others held for murder broke jail and fled toward Old Mexico. The sheriff identified by Fourr as Joseph Phy trailed the "sack thief" across the international boundary, captured him, and started back to Tucson. On American soil once more, the tired sheriff fell asleep, and the killer again escaped back into Mexico. This time Phy hired another Mexican to track the "sack thief" down and bring him back, which he did. Phy had the satisfaction of delivering the killer to Yuma prison, but V. M. and the other escapees were never caught.

The reminiscences of Charley Harrison have those of another bloody encounter at Blue Water Station. Traveling with one Fred Anderson from Tucson to Montezuma, again presumed to be the store of that name, they arrived at Blue Water to find that the hostler or station keeper at that time and a Mexican family of five who lived there had been killed by Apaches. The slaughter had taken place so recently that the bodies were still warm, and all had been scalped. Anderson was all for fleeing immediately, but Harrison sent him away to a place he called Mano Pochi or "Manos Porchus" (meaning "short hand") to bring back a posse while Harrison stayed at the station.

In two hours Anderson was back with 20 men armed with muskets and carbines. They took up the trail of the Indians. Within an hour they unexpectedly came upon the Indians going into camp, and after a sharp fight killed them all. The posse dug a shallow trench and buried the bodies of the Indians, something that was not always done. Harrison concludes by saying that he and Anderson started back to Tucson to report to the military, but chanced to run into an army patrol led by a Lieutenant Irvin, to whom they made their report, and went on their way.

From Blue Water the Butterfield Trail swung northward toward the Pima Villages on the Gila River. The next station was only some 20 miles from Blue Water. It was called the Oneida Station, where teams were changed only. Again nothing remains of it and there is a plowed field where it was. Little is known of it and it is likely that the station existed only for a short time. Billy Fourr's reference to the Oneida station the first time he passed it, probably in 1862 or 1863, was that the station was deserted and there was no water.

From Oneida the trail led northward between the Sacaton Mountains and Thin Mountain to McClellan Wash, down which it then ran to the Pima village of Sacaton near the Gila River. The Butterfield agent here was Hiram Stevens, the first trader to establish a store on the Gila River Indian Reservation (1859), in this village. Sacaton is almost universally considered the oldest and most enduring of the Pima villages along the Gila. It became the agency and tribal headquarters of the reservation and remains so today. The number of Pima and Maricopa villages in the mid-1800s was about 10, the number of them and their names varying with whose list was consulted. Those definitely on or near the Butterfield trail by historical accounts were Sacaton and Casa Blanca, where another station was located, Sweetwater, and Sacate.

The Pima and Maricopa Indians who occupied these villages were the complete opposite of the nomadic, warlike and merciless Apaches who were despised and feared by settlers and travelers alike. Pimas and Maricopas were peaceful and friendly, their villages oases of rest and regeneration from the harsh rigors of the overland trail. These industrious tribes had lived for centuries along the Gila, watering their farms from miles of hand-dug canals taking water from the river. They grew large acreages of wheat, pumpkins, squash, beans and other food crops, much of which was sold or traded to the whites. Almost without exception, they were generous, kind and helpful to travelers, whose accounts of that day are filled with praise for them.

While peaceful by nature, the Pima and Maricopa warriors were second to none in courage and fighting ability when attacked. Their hereditary enemies were the warlike Yuma and Hualapai Indians who lived along the Colorado River to the west, and the Apaches to the east, whom they hated with a fervor as deep as the whites. The Pimas and Maricopas vigorously defended their homes and fields from the Apaches who raided them regularly, and went on retaliatory raids against their old enemy. Huge battles, lasting for days, fought mostly with war clubs, were reported in encounters with the Yumas and

Hualapais, after which the ground was said to be littered with the dead of both tribes. After the Civil War, many Pima and Maricopa warriors served as scouts for the American military in its campaigns against the Apaches.

From Sacaton, the Butterfield trail roughly following the course of the Gila ran westward passing near Sweetwater to Casa Blanca, about ten miles distant. On the west of present-day Casa Blanca about a mile-and-a-half was the store of trader Ammi White, where the Butterfield station was located. White, the reservation's first resident agent, also had a flour mill which turned out large quantities of flour, and large storehouses of wheat and corn bought from the Indian farmers. His store and mill was the location of the westernmost of two encounters between Union and Confederate forces during the Civil War.

With the outbreak of the war, Capt. Sherod Hunter had been sent with 200 Texans by the Confederacy to occupy Tucson and secure the territory for the South. The Union raised a force of 1800 men, known as the "California Column," which under Col. James H. Carleton advanced eastward from Yuma on the Gila trail early in 1862. Carleton sent Capt. William McCleave ahead with a scouting party, and Billy Fourr tells how it was captured at Ammi White's store by the Confederates, ranging westward along the trail from Tucson.

Fourr's account is that the Confederate patrol heard from the Indians that the Union force was advancing, and concealed itself in White's corral, intending to make a fight of it. Unaware that the Southern force was so near, McCleave had his Union force go into camp and stack arms 300 or 400 yards west of the store. McCleave and his sergeant walked into the store, where they were immediately surrounded and disarmed by Confederate soldiers. The rest of the Confederates then merely walked into the Union camp where the guns were stacked, ordering the completely surprised soldiers to surrender, which they did without firing a shot. McCleave and his soldiers were escorted east as prisoners of war, and trader Ammi White was arrested as a Union sympathizer and jailed in Tucson.

Though the Southern force of Hunter retired eastward in May 1862, in the face of the Union's numerical superiority, for some reason White remained in the Tucson bastille. Probably it was because Tucsonans of that day were predominantly sympathetic to the Southern cause. It was not until Arizona's

Ruins of original Mohawk Station on the Butterfield Trail. Photo made in 1972. (Conkling Collection, Courtesy Arizona Historical Society)

first governor, John Goodwin, appointed Coles Bashford to be Attorney General on February 1, 1864, and ordered him to look into Ammi White's case, that relief was forthcoming. White was ordered released from jail. Understandably miffed, White left Arizona after selling his flour mill to the Bichard Brothers, who moved it to Adamsville, four miles south of Florence and now a ghost town.

From Casa Blanca the Butterfield trail gradually swung toward the Gila River only a short distance away, passed the village of Sacate and, almost on the river's bank, rounded the base of Pima Butte to continue to Maricopa Wells station some three miles beyond. From this point it would be necessary, in order to avoid the arduous travel in following the Gila River making a sweeping curve to the north, to travel across the Forty-Mile Desert to rejoin the river again where it made its last great bend westward. Wagon trains and military columns of all kinds had to load up enough water here to last for that 40 miles. Maricopa Wells for this reason and others became the most important and busiest station on the Butterfield route and those that succeeded it. It was at the half-way point across Arizona, was on the intersection of the east-west Gila trail with the only north-south trail through central Arizona, and in 1865 became the supply point on the trail for Fort McDowell when it was established on the Verde River to the northeast. A subsequent chapter will be devoted to this station on the line.

From Maricopa Wells, the last of the relatively secure places near the Pima villages, the trail ran across the desert with its perils actually increasing from Apache raiders from the north, Yuma and Hualapai Indians from the west, and Mexican bandits and outlaws ranging northward from Sonora. Halfway across the Forty-Mile Desert the Butterfield company established Desert Station. The station itself was constructed of adobe, and was a change station only, where teams pulling the coaches were changed. There was a dug well of limited capacity, and most of the water was hauled 20 miles one way or the other, from Maricopa Wells or the next station on the line at the Gila River bend, Gila Ranch Station.

The Butterfield trail reached the Gila River again where it made its big bend westerly around the end of the Gila Bend Mountains. On the riverbank opposite the mountains the Gila Ranch station was built in 1858. This was a time station as well as a team change station; drivers were expected to arrive and leave Gila Ranch at certain times to keep the line on schedule.

About 20 miles west of Gila Ranch, the next station was first known as Murderer's Grave. In 1854 travelers on the trail were camped on the spot, when a young man went berserk and killed his guardian. Other travelers camped there were so incensed that they hanged the murderer on the spot, and buried both victims alongside the road. This name was changed later to Kenyon's Station, named for a man named Marcus Kenyon then in charge of that section of the line. After Butterfield ceased operations and the Civil War had come and gone, the old station was still in use by other lines. Billy Fourr recounts the murder there on August 18, 1873, of Edward Lumley, the station keeper at the time. Lumley's partner, John Murphy, was running the Oatman Flat station further west at that time, both of which the men leased. The incident followed a recurring pattern in which the station keepers were overpowered, tortured to make them reveal the location of money and valuables, then murdered. Then the murderers, be they Apache, renegade Mexicans or white outlaws fled with their loot, sometimes to escape and sometimes to be caught and brought to some kind of justice.

Fourr, who was leasing his Oatman Flat station to these men and himself farming near Gila Bend, had chased away two Mexicans he caught stealing watermelons. In a few days the Mexicans, who later were identified as Lucas Lugas and Manuel Subiate, were camped near Kenyon's Station. When Lumley went to his henhouse to gather eggs, he was struck on the back of the head and knocked down by the Mexican desperados, who then tied his hand around a mesquite tree. Lumley was tortured to get him to tell where his money was hidden, stabbed eleven times with a knife, and his head finally bashed in with a rock. The killer fled with the usual booty, horses, guns, saddles and bridles, other articles and $50 in cash. No less a personage than Governor Anson Safford, with a man named Theo F. White, passed by the station before Lumley's body was buried, and passed on the details to other authorities.

Westward along the Gila trail the murderers fled, where near Yuma the sheriff picked up their trail. The two men crossed the Colorado River as did the sheriff, who succeeded in capturing Subiate, but Lugas escaped. The sheriff chanced upon two California boys, told them about the fleeing man, and said he would give a $500 reward for his capture. The boys tracked the Mexican through the brush and wounded him with a shotgun blast. The next morning with another man they set out to follow the bloody trail, which came to an arrowweed thicket. With the boys on horseback on the riverbank above, the man started into the thicket and was charged by the Mexican carrying a big knife. The boys shot and killed the murderer, picked up the knife which proved to be the one that killed Lumley, and collected the reward.

The sheriff of Maricopa County, Tom Hayes, went to Yuma to return the prisoner to Phoenix to stand trial. Traveling back with his prisoner by stagecoach, Hayes became apprehensive when approaching Kenyon's Station that there might be trouble with some of Lumley's friends. It was about one o'clock in the morning, and under cover of night, Hayes and his prisoner dropped off the stagecoach shortly before it reached Kenyon's, the sheriff instructing the driver that they would reboard the coach on the other side of the station.

At the station, 20 well-armed vigilantes, waiting for the stagecoach, forced the driver to reveal the actions and instructions of the sheriff. They then took over the stagecoach themselves, substituting one of their own as driver, the rest following behind. The darkness made resistance impossible, the sheriff was forced to remove the prisoner's shackles and turn him over to the vigilantes. The killer was taken back to Kenyon's Station and hanged to a mesquite tree within sight of the henhouse. Hayes returned to Phoenix to recount what had occurred. The grand jury, waiting to hand down an indictment, immediately dispersed. Lumley's grave, the marker erected by his partner Murphy, and the old station have long since been obliterated by floods along the Gila.

West of Kenyon's 14 miles a station was established at Oatman Flat. This spot was named for the emigrant Oatman family, most of whom were murdered there by Yavapai Indians in 1851. It is said that in Butterfield days the stage route ran directly over the common grave of the Oatman family. In 1874 the Oatman Flat station, which had been abandoned for some time because the road had deteriorated, was taken over by Billy Fourr who had married the daughter of an emigrating Texas family. Fourr spent $5,000 repairing the road that ran past the station, and was given a toll road charter by the legislature, allowing him to charge for using the road, to thus get his money back. Fourr remarked that a shotgun was better than the charter for collecting the tolls, but people were so reluctant to pay that he never recovered all that he had spent. Fourr also established a ranch, and at Oatman Flat are still to be found the ruins of the ranch house, graves of the children of the Fourrs who died in infancy, and a monument to the Oatman family.

Thirteen miles west of Oatman Flat, Burk's station operated by Patrick Burk was established in 1858. "Burk" is the authentic spelling, though some sources add an "e." In later years this station had also been operated by Billy Fourr, who sold it early in July 1874, to G. R. Whistler. The new owner employed a Ventura Nunez to clean out the well. When he had been paid for his work, the Mexican asked of Whistler the price of an item in the store. When Whistler turned to check, the Mexican shot him in the back, killing him. This murder took place on July 7, 1874. Nunez with his loot from the station fled toward the Mexican border with Billy Fourr on his trail. A prominent Arizonan named King Woolsey with some of his men caught up with Fourr, and on July 9th, 60 miles south of the station, Fourr and Woolsey and his men captured the fleeing Nunez.

Nunez was stopped with a shot in the leg. The wounded man was taken back to the station where, according to the accounts,

Original Filibuster Camp stage station, 22 miles east of Yuma on the Butterfield Overland Trail. (Courtesy Arizona Historical Society)

a group of citizens of the surrounding area had gathered. They established the guilt of the murderer, who then confessed. He was forthwith hanged to a mesquite tree in front of the station and the body allowed to dangle as a warning to any others with such notions, until it deteriorated and fell to the ground, when it was buried by some passing Mexican traders.

The next station west of Oatman Flat on the Butterfield trail was Stanwick's Station operated by a man of that name. It was also called Flat Creek Station, Flapjack Ranch and Stanwix, appearing on some maps with that spelling. It was after the Butterfield route had ceased operations, however, that the station became best known. In 1861 or early in 1862 the abandoned station was taken over and renovated by one of Arizona's celebrated pioneers, King S. Woolsey. A diligent man, Woolsey not only ran the station but started a large farming operation. He contracted with the government to supply hay and mesquite beans to the military, though Woolsey himself was sympathetic to the South.

An incident told of Woolsey is that one day, away from the station, he was harvesting hay with some of his employees when they were suddenly set upon by a band of Tonto Apaches. Woolsey and his men had with them only a loaded double-barreled shotgun. As the Indians rushed to the attack, Woolsey fired one barrel of the gun to attempt to scare them off, but the range was too great and the charge fell harmlessly. With shouts of defiance, the Indians crept closer, urged on by their chief, a huge and powerful warrior. Waiting until the chief was within range, Woolsey shot him in the head with the charge in the other barrel, stopping the Indian attack. In the confusion, Woolsey and his men unhitched the mules from the hay wagon and fled back to the station for weapons and reinforcements. When they returned to the battle, the Apaches had fled, leaving the dead chief's body. It was taken back to the station and hung to a mesquite tree where, shot full of arrows by passing Pimas and Maricopas, it stayed until it deteriorated and fell to the ground.

Prospering from his station serving travelers on the trail, his farms and his government contracts, Woolsey in 1862 bought the Agua Caliente ranch across the Gila a short distance from the station, with a partner, George Martin, whose interest he later acquired. There a hot spring flowed from the ground at the site of a former Maricopa Indian village, and there Woolsey began a ranching operation where his home was famous for his hospitality throughout the territory. He was a popular and powerful leader in territorial Arizona, the terror of Indians and Mexican bandits.

There are, however, two cases of tragic mistaken identity on record. In 1872 Sheriff T. C. Warden captured Ramon Cordova who was known as "the Yaqui bandit" at Agua Caliente. Cordova was suspected of being in on the stagecoach holdup and murder of its occupants known as the "Wickenburg massacre." He was thrown into jail and then lynched. It was eventually proved that the massacre of the stagecoach passengers was the work of Hualapai Indians from the Date Creek reservation near Prescott. The other instance was the mistaken identity of a man accused of being one Chavez, a highwayman who had operated in California. Two of Woolsey's herders identified a man working on a Gila River ranch as Chavez, who attempted to flee, and was shot down by another of Woolsey's men. The body was taken in a wagon to Yuma, where it was declared not to be that of Chavez after all.

West of Stanwick's on the Butterfield route another 15 miles was Grinnell's Station, kept by Henry Grinnell, built of adobe in 1858. Little seems to be known about this station, and in the years after Butterfield went out of business it was replaced by a station identified by John Crampton as "Painted Rocks." Presumably there were ancient Indian petroglyphs scratched in the rocks near this station, of which again little seems to be known. This station was also known as Texas Hill.

Eleven miles west of Grinnell's Station was the next of the adobe stations built in 1858, Peterman's Station, also named for the keeper. Again little is known of Peterman's during the Butterfield days, but in later years another was built at this site to serve other stage lines and freighters. It was called Mohawk Station, after the valley in which it was situated and some nearby mountains in turn named by passing emigrants from New York state. In 1871 Mohawk Station was owned by a man whose name is variously spelled John Killbride, Killbright and Kilbright, who had previously owned the Mission Camp Station further west. According to the memoirs of John F. Crampton, Kilbright committed suicide by taking a dose of poison, then jumping into the well. A short time later one of the teams ran away and also plunged into the well, after which Crampton notes a new well had to be dug.

Following the death of Kilbright, a man named Peck, with his wife, took over the station. Peck had a flock of chickens, and about a hundred Sonora goats that he had brought from Mexico, and with a couple of Angora bucks was breeding them up. It is almost certainly about Peck and his wife that the following was written by an anonymous army officer. This account first appeared in the *Los Angeles Star* and was reprinted in the *Journal of the West*:

> Arriving at this camp, we pitched our tents and got our supper... The station consists of one adobe house covered by a roof of brush. This ranch is occupied by a man who, even in this desert wilderness, can boast of a wife to share with him his unenviable solitude. Their chief means of support is the sale of "tarantula juice" and other such scanty merchantable articles as can be obtained in this barren country.
>
> They cooked a chicken for us which was burnt so badly that it would have made an excellent tonic for fever or ague, so far as the bitter properties were concerned... Notwithstanding the very rough company with which our hostess is constantly surrounded, and the fact that the nearest neighbor of her sex lives at Yuma, 40 miles distant, she seems to accept her lot with great cheerfulness... As I write, the hostess is sitting on a sack of barley, while her husband is behind the bar to attend to any thirsty wants of the company—which consists of soldiers, drivers, Mexicans, miners, herders, and trampers, most of whom, to judge from their appearance, make the study of cutting a throat the principal business of their lives.

The next station west of Peterman's on the original Butterfield route was 18 miles distant and called Filibuster Camp. Built of adobe in 1858, this station was closed in 1859 and moved six miles east to Antelope Peak which had a better water supply. Crampton's memoirs state that the Antelope Peak station "was kept by A. Hewitt, where Brown, a member of the California Volunteers, in 1865 shot and killed his wife. The lonely grave was right alongside of the stage road." In later years, however, Filibuster Camp was rebuilt. It was at this site that the private army of "General" Henry A. Crabb assembled in 1857 to undertake an expedition into Mexico. In return for helping a Mexican rebel come to power, Crabb was to receive a strip of land between Sonora and the United States. An account of the bloody history of this ill-fated expedition is told in another chapter.

Mission Camp, an original station on the Butterfield Overland route, was built in 1858 but was also closed in 1859 with the opening of the station at Antelope Peak. Mission Camp was said to have been built at a site where there were ruins of an old Spanish mission, possibly that mentioned in the writings of the famed Father Eusebio Kino as having been established by him 100 years previously. Following the Civil War this station was rebuilt to serve other stage lines, the work reported to have been done by the John Kilbright mentioned in connection with Mohawk Station.

According to Crampton's memoirs, Kilbright sold the station to one Peter Reed early in December 1870. On December 24 the station was suddenly attacked by Mexican bandits, who had killed Reed and stage driver, James Lytle, chopped off the head of the cook, Thomas Oliver, with an axe, and had Mrs. Reed by the hair when an inspection party unexpectedly drove up. In the party were a Col. Hinton, Dave Gibson, Charles Kenyon, and James A Moore, superintendent of the stage line. They saved Mrs. Reed from the murderers, who fled and made good their escape into Mexico only 30 miles to the south.

The last of Butterfield's Arizona stations was established in 1858 in the ranch home of Jacob Snively, 13 miles west of Mission Camp, and called Snivelly's Station. In November of that year Snivelly discovered rich deposits of placer gold along the Gila River nearby, and there ensued Arizona Territory's first true gold rush. Within a few weeks hundreds of men swarmed over the area, staking claims and washing out deposits of gold. At the ranch Gila City sprang up, but it consisted of only a half-dozen permanent adobe buildings, the rest tents and other temporary shelters. Gradually the gold and the population dwindled, though some kept trying for years, but by 1865 Gila City was practically deserted again. By 1872 there was only a house, a stable and a corral.

To the *Los Angeles Star* the army officer correspondent reported in 1872:

> Gila City consists of one adobe house in which reside two men who keep the stage station, wash gold from a gulch close by and sell lightning whiskey to anyone who can drink it. We pitched our tents in the center of the town, which is to say between the house before-mentioned and the mule corral about 200 rods distant. We boiled our coffee and sat down to a good dinner from our mess chest. . . The mules were driven to the river for water. . .
>
> A caravan of Mexicans, men, women and children, mounted on donkeys came by, on one of which animals sat a large Mexican, astride, while from a couple of large baskets on either side stuckup the heads of two brown-faced children—the only pleasant feature of the caravan. The women were enveloped in shawls and did not disclose their faces. The men look the bandit to perfection. Our sentinel is posted at dusk, the mules are corralled, and we turn into our tents. . .

Jacob Snivelly, station keeper and founder of Gila City, was later killed by Indians while prospecting in central Arizona. Snivelly's Station was the last of the original Butterfield stations in Arizona. Westward 22 miles was the Colorado River, where stagecoaches crossed on a ferry to Fort Yuma, then on the California side, and Yates Stage Station. In later years a station would be established on the Arizona side at the home of Louis F. Jaeger in Colorado City, forerunner of the City of Yuma.

The building of the railroad across southern Arizona in the last years of the 1870s forced the old trail and its stations into the romantic mysteries of the West. Even the railroads and highways that replaced it followed the old trail closely, some-times alongside it for long miles, sometimes directly over it and the station sites. Still today, in places where the old trail was by-passed it can be seen, even traveled, over ruts worn deeply by thousands of passing wheels. In Apache Pass, over the north end of the Dragoon Mountains, across the Forty-Mile Desert and along the Gila traces of the old trail can be discerned by returnees to Arizona's Old West.

CHAPTER 2
Apache Pass

Twenty-five miles west of the border of New Mexico, sixty miles north of the border of Old Mexico, the southern emigrant trail that later became the Butterfield Overland trail ran into mountains. To the south were the rugged Chiricahua Mountains extending almost all the way to the border; to the west towered the rough Dos Cabezas desert range with its distinctive feature resembling two heads that gave it its Spanish name. Beyond was the flat, open, high desert of the Sulphur Springs Valley. There was one trail through the foothills between these mountain ranges, a rough and winding ten-mile defile known as Apache Pass. Near the southern end of the pass was a year-round spring, Apache Spring, always with an abundance of precious water. Apache Pass, then, was a vital and vulnerable link in the trail.

The pass became vulnerable at the whims of the Apache Indians. Approaching Arizona Territory from the east, travelers had passed through the territories of the nomadic and warlike Mimbres Apaches and the Warm Springs Apaches who were bad enough. At Apache Pass they crossed the territory of the fiercest and most dreaded of all the Apache tribes, the Chiricahua Apaches. The history of the struggle for domination of this pass is as dramatic and bloody as any in the saga of the West. It was decided not by raw courage and reckless bravery, which both whites and Apaches demonstrated in abundance, but by superior arms.

Apaches and Americans were not always at odds. The first Americans to enter the area were looked upon by the Apaches as sort of allies against the Mexicans, with whom the Americans were at war. The Apaches had been at war with the Mexicans for two hundred years, and both sides thoroughly despised the other. Spanish and then Mexican attempts to pacify the Apaches by force of arms, then a campaign of extermination, had failed. The Apaches had answered through the years with campaigns of slaughter of their own, and American battles with the Mexicans gave the Indians respite from the Mexican military. When the Americans supplanted the Mexicans, however, the Apaches soon found them little if any better than the Mexicans. The Apaches bitterly resented and resisted the

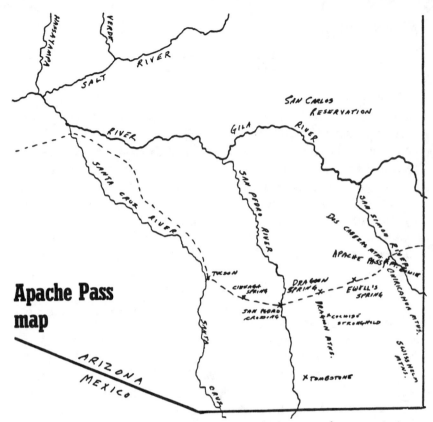

Apache Pass map

incursions into lands that had been their own, and attempts to round them up and force them onto reservations. The history of treaties made and broken, and atrocities by both sides, is well documented.

When the Butterfield route was laid out through Apache Pass, the chief of the Chiricahua Apaches was the great Cochise. Then in his forties and a giant among Apaches in stature and intellect, Cochise had always kept the peace with the Americans. That does not mean that there were not incidents, raids and killings, instigated by both sides, but generally Cochise kept the Chiricahua Apaches at peace. He felt that it was better to get along with the Americans and bedevil the Apaches' ancient enemies in Mexico. Butterfield representatives made agreements with the old chief, furnishing him with trade goods in exchange for promises that the stagecoaches would travel in safety. From the line's inception until early in 1861, no stagecoach was attacked by the Chiricahua Apaches. In fact, during this period all traffic moved through Apache Pass safe from their attacks.

In October 1860, some Indians raided the ranch of one John Ward on Sonoita Creek, running off some stock and carrying away Ward's half-Indian son. This boy would one day become the well-known scout for the military, Mickey Free. Ward kept after the military to find the boy, and in January 1861, soldiers under Lieutenant George Bascom were sent out on this mission from Fort Buchanan. Entering Apache Pass from the west, Bascom and his fifty-four men passed the stagecoach station a half-mile from Apache Spring and camped about a mile from the station, in Siphon Draw. A squaw who was at the station carried the news to Cochise, camped in the hills above the pass.

Bascom and his force had moved into the lands of the Chiricahua Apaches at the suspicions of Ward that Indians from this tribe had carried out the raid on his ranch. Though he was really looking for Cochise's band, Bascom had let it be known that he was merely traveling eastward on a military mission. When the chief, then, decided to visit the military camp he was entirely unsuspecting of the true nature of Bascom's expedition and simply walked into his hands. Taking a half-brother, two nephews, his wife and small son with him, Cochise went to visit Bascom's camp. This was on February 3, 1861.

When the Indians entered Bascom's tent, it was immediately surrounded by soldiers. Bascom, only two years out of West Point and unfamiliar with Apache ways, stated his mission. Cochise replied that he knew nothing of the raid, that it had not been carried out by members of his tribe, but that he would investigate and help find the boy and recover the stolen stock. Bascom then made the first of a series of terrible mistakes. He accused Cochise of lying and announced that all of his visitors were prisoners and would remain so until Ward's son was returned.

Cochise whipped out a knife that had been concealed in his breech clout, slashed through the tent, darted past the surprised soldiers, and escaped through the chaparral without being touched by the bullets fired at him. His relatives were all detained as prisoners. By fires and smoke signals Cochise called in his warriors. Bascom moved his camp to the stagecoach station. On February 5th, Cochise approached the station with a large band of braves under a white flag. Bascom and some soldiers moved out to talk with Cochise, but suspiciously kept their distance. Not so some of the Butterfield employees, who knew Cochise well. Suddenly the Apaches rushed three Butterfield men, capturing a stage driver, James Wallace, killing one and wounding one of two others who fled amid an exchange of gunfire between the Apaches and soldiers.

Later that day a train of freight wagons entered Apache Pass from the west. The Apaches attacked and destroyed it, taking two hostages and torturing eight Mexicans whom they tied to wagon wheels and burned to death. The next day Cochise again approached the station. The captured stage driver, Wallace, hands bound to a rope tied to Cochise's saddle, spoke the Apache tongue and interpreted the chief's offer to exchange his three prisoners and some stolen mules for Cochise's relatives held by Bascom. Bascom replied that no exchange would take place unless the Ward boy was included. Cochise repeated that he had no knowledge of the boy or his whereabouts. Wallace begged Bascom to reconsider, but he refused over the objections of one of his sergeants so strong that he had the man placed under arrest. Cochise then dragged Wallace to death behind his galloping horse.

Fort Bowie circa 1880s, looking southward toward Helen's Dome. The last Apache band to surrender, under Geronimo, was held here before being sent to exile in Florida in 1886. (Courtesy Arizona Historical Society)

Bascom sent dispatches describing the situation to Tucson and to Fort Breckenridge, which were delivered. The Apaches piled rocks, and brush which they planned to set afire, in the trail through the pass intending to ambush the stagecoaches. The westbound stagecoach arrived early and escaped the ambush. The eastbound stage was fired upon just after entering the pass, killing one of the lead mules and badly wounding the driver. The mule was cut out of the harness under heavy fire, and a Butterfield official named Buckley drove the stagecoach to the safety of the station in Apache Pass where another of the mules dropped dead in its harness.

Soldiers from Fort Buchanan arrived to reinforce Bascom, and in searching for Cochise came upon the bodies of the Mexicans still tied to the wagon wheels, and of Wallace and two other hostages who had been tortured to death and mutilated beyond recognition. For ten days the soldiers scouted the mountains around the pass, burned some abandoned Apache rancherias, but found none to fight since the Indians had scattered to their strongholds to watch the soldiers and the trail below. On February 19th the soldiers withdrew from the pass to return to Fort Buchanan. As they did so, they hanged three Coyotero Apaches captured by soldiers reinforcing Bascom and three of Cochise's relatives, sparing only the woman and her child, retaliation for the tortures and murders by the Apaches.

The already infuriated Cochise was only further inflamed by this gesture of defiance and vengeance by the departing soldiers. He declared war upon the Americans as murderous and bloodthirsty as any the Apaches had ever waged against the Mexicans. Watching from their posts on the peaks along the trail through Apache Pass, they attacked anything that entered it, killing, torturing, looting and burning. For a time traffic through the pass was completely halted. It is said that in later years, when traveling through the pass, one was never out of sight of the wreckage of vehicles and the bleaching bones of men and animals.

While the preceding account of the Bascom affair is the one that is generally accepted, there is a dissenting opinion as so often is the case in Arizona history, which should not be ignored. The opinion is that of Constance Wynn Altshuler, a writer who took an interest in dispatches from Arizona to a San Francisco newspaper, the **Bulletin.** The correspondent was called "Hesperian," a pen-name meaning "Westerner," whom Altshuler identified as T. M. Turner, once editor of the Tucson *Citizen.* Her book, *Latest from Arizona: The Hesperian Letters, 1859-1861* published by the Arizona Historical Society in 1969, analyzed the letters, comparing them with official military and other records.

Altshuler maintains that the sergeant mentioned as having objected so strongly to Bascom's treatment of Cochise that he was put under arrest was not even there at that time. Reuben F. Bernard, who enlisted as a private and rose through the ranks to become a general officer, was a first sergeant of dragoons at this time, and Bascom had no dragoons in his command. Altshuler states that Bernard arrived with the dragoons in the relief column from Fort Buchanan, and that he invented his part in the Bascom affair in a speech given in Tucson after the war. His version was repeated so often, she says, that it became accepted as fact. In his official report, however, Bascom made no mention of arresting a non-commissioned officer, but commended all of them, without exception, for their conduct during the mission.

Altshuler's version also differs on a few other points, one being that the stage driver, Wallace, was not dragged to death behind Cochise's horse, but that his body was found with those of three other captives, freighters William Sanders, Frank Brunner and Sam Whitfield, all killed by several stab wounds with a lance. Another difference is her suggestion that Cochise did not escape Bascom's custody amid flying bullets, but was allowed to leave to find the missing boy while his relatives were held as hostages. These are major variances from the details of the usual version, an example of many to be found in accounts of Arizona history.

Two months after the unfortunate Bascom incident, the Civil War broke out. Military posts in Arizona were closed and the soldiers sent eastward to fight for the Union. Seeing the soldiers leaving, the Apaches thought that they had won the fight and redoubled their efforts to drive the white man from their lands. They attacked little settlements at ranches and mines, now without protection of any kind, killing, burning, driving off stock. Only at a few fortified places, such as Tucson, to which the Americans fled for mutual protection were they able to hold out against the warring Apaches.

In February 1862, a force of two hundred Texans under Captain Sherod Hunter occupied Tucson to hold Arizona for the Confederacy. To counter this, the Union raised a force of 1,800 men in California, called the "California Column." Under Brigadier General James H. Carleton this army marched eastward toward Tucson. In the face of superior numbers, Hunter retired back to Texas, and the California Column marched into Tucson in May 1862. Carleton's orders were to continue eastward to New Mexico and secure it for the Union. The Californians marched along the old emigrant and Butterfield trail, and at Dragoon Spring on the north slope of the Dragoon Mountains camped while an advance force moved forward to secure the water supply at Apache Spring. Already the California Column was suffering casualties as the Apaches attacked detachments, hunting parties and couriers.

Leaving Capt. John Cremony at Dragoon Spring, Capt. Thomas Roberts advanced into Apache Pass with 126 men to secure the water supply at Apache Spring. Unknown to him, Cochise was waiting for him in ambush with six hundred warriors of a combined force of his own Chiricahua Apaches and Warm Springs Apaches under their chief, Mangas Coloradas. Barely into the pass the soldiers came under heavy fire, retreated to regroup, and re-entered the pass. Along the old Butterfield stage trail they fought their way toward Apache Spring, where they found the Indians entrenched behind natural rock breastworks. Roberts was fortunate to have with him two small howitzers, and shells from these guns forced the Indians from their positions. The troopers then took possession of the spring.

Roberts sent six couriers back to Cremony telling him that the troopers would return to Dragoon Spring, leaving a force to hold Apache Spring, to escort the supply wagons through the pass. Barely out of the pass, the couriers were attacked by forty Apaches and engaged in a running fight. A Private John Teal's horse was killed, and from behind its body he fought the Indians alone. He shot Mangas Coloradas himself in the chest, whereupon the Indians broke off the engagement, and Teal was able to walk back to join Cremony's command. A Mexican doctor was forced to remove the bullet from the chest of Mangas Coloradas, who lived to be captured and killed by soldiers at Fort Bayard.

Roberts' fight at Apache Spring took place July 15, 1862. On

July 16, his men marched back to Dragoon Spring and escorted the wagons into Apache Pass, where they found that the Apaches had re-occupied their positions during the night. Once more the howitzers scattered them. On July 17th Roberts continued through the pass, reporting back to General Carleton, following, that in the two-day battle he had two killed, two wounded, and had killed nine Indians. He was only saved from extermination by the cannon, however, and recommended that a military post be established in Apache Pass to escort travelers through it and to guard the water at the spring.

Carleton arrived with the main body of the California Column at Apache Pass on July 27th. After inspecting the terrain and conditions there, he completely agreed with Roberts' assessment that a fort must be built and permanently manned to hold the pass against the Apaches. At his order a fort was built on a hill overlooking Apache Spring, about a mile from the trail through the pass. Soldiers were left behind, when Carleton advanced to New Mexico, to build and man the fort. It was named Fort Bowie after the commander of the Fifth Infantry, Col. George W. Bowie.

The fort actually consisted of a rock wall some 400 feet long surrounding the post area, in which the soldiers mainly lived in tents. In time it was moved to a more desirable location nearby, and its facilities upgraded to those of a permanent installation,

Ruins of Fort Bowie, Apache Pass, 1987.

but it was always considered an unhappy assignment by those stationed there. It had its effect, however, since the Apaches never again controlled the pass or the spring. Building the post's permanent facilities was an additional duty for the soldiers who escorted freight wagon trains, travelers and mail couriers through the pass and engaged in sorties against the Apaches until after the Civil War when they were relieved by infantry and cavalry of the regular army.

With the Civil War at an end, Fort Bowie became an important post along with such other new places as Fort Huachuca, Fort McDowell and Fort Apache in dealing with the Indians. Cochise continued his warfare against white settlers and travelers unabated, and a succession of departmental and post commanders took the field against him. One of the post commanders at Fort Bowie was Capt. Reuben F. Bernard, once the sergeant who had been arrested by Lt. Bascom in 1861 for protesting his treatment of Cochise, now risen through the ranks to become an officer. Later in his career Bernard became a general officer. While at Bowie from 1869 to 1871 he was continually on the trail of Cochise and his Apaches, fighting and killing them in a number of engagements. Far from being subjugated, Cochise's Apaches continued to raid and plunder at will on both sides of the Mexican border, scattering to their hideouts in the mountain fastnesses when presented by troops.

In 1872 General O. O. Howard succeeded in making peace with Cochise. A white rancher and sometimes government scout named Tom Jeffords had made friends with the old chief in 1867 by his fearlessness in walking alone into Cochise's camp and asking for peace for himself and his family. In an Apache ceremony Cochise and Jeffords had become 'blood brothers,' and the Apaches never molested Jeffords. Gen. Howard asked Jeffords to guide him to Cochise's camp, and Jeffords agreed if the general would go without soldiers at his back. In September 1872, Jeffords and two Apache scouts Jeffords knew to be in Cochise's favor led the general and his aide across the Sulphur Springs Valley to Cochise's stronghold in the Dragoon Mountains. There the general met Cochise and stayed for ten days to arrange peace with the Chiricahua Apaches.

Cochise called in his war chiefs and sub-chiefs to discuss the terms of the peace, and their discussions and arguments were long and bitter. At length with the wide powers given him

Howard agreed to establish a reservation for the Chiricahua Apaches taking in the Chiricahua and Dragoon mountain ranges and large parts of the San Simon Valley to the east, the Sulphur Springs Valley and the San Pedro Valley to the west, on stipulation by the Apaches that Tom Jeffords would be the Indian agent. Jeffords strenuously objected, but when faced with the fact that there would be no peace treaty unless he accepted, he did so.

The Chiricahua Apaches kept the peace treaty inviolate from 1872 until the death of Cochise in 1876. Jeffords had no trouble with them, for they liked and trusted him, but he had nothing but trouble from the whites. Ranchers and settlers were unhappy with the reservation boundaries, military men were bitterly jealous, and suppliers constantly cheated the Indians and furnished them with the strictly forbidden whiskey. Jeffords moved the tribal agency from Sulphur Springs to San Simon to Pinery Canyon and finally into Apache Pass itself in attempts to solve the reservation's problems.

With Cochise's death went his iron control over his people. The chiefdom passed to his son Taza, who continued to cooperate with Jeffords, but whose hold over the tribe was never as strong as his father's and gradually slipped away. Sub-chiefs favoring going back to war with the whites gradually gained in power, and in the face of all these pressures the Bureau of Indian Affairs ordered the ouster of Jeffords and the removal of the Chiricahua Apaches to the San Carlos reservation to the north. On June 12, 1876, Taza and 325 of his tribesmen left Apache Pass for San Carlos escorted by Agent John Clum and troops from Fort Bowie. Renegade Apache bands under their war chiefs fled into the mountains. The Chiricahua Reservation was abolished and restored to the public domain.

Once more the war chiefs of the Chiricahua Apaches led their followers on bloody raids against American and Mexican settlements, ranches and travelers. Such chiefs as Geronimo, Juh, Natchez, Loco and Chato slipped back and forth between the comparative safety of the San Carlos reservation and their hideouts in the Sierra Madre Mountains of Old Mexico, raiding and killing and plundering as they went. A succession of military commanders pursued them, notably General George Crook and General Nelson Miles. It was another ten years before attrition and defections wore down the Apaches and ended the warfare with the surrender of the last band of hostiles under Geronimo to General Miles at Skeleton Canyon in September 1886.

After Geronimo's surrender, his band was taken to Fort Bowie and detained there. One morning the Apaches were assembled on the parade ground and loaded into wagons, as the soldiers of the command stood at attention in parade formation. The wagons, escorted by soldiers under Captain Henry Lawton, proceeded along the wagon road through Apache Pass to the railroad siding of Bowie, where the Apaches were put on a train. They were exiled to Florida, where the climate proved to be so unhealthful for them that many became ill and died. The rest were moved to Alabama, and eventually to Fort Sill in what is now Oklahoma where they remained, and near where many of their descendents lived.

For a time following Geronimo's surrender Apache Pass was a busy place, with military activity centered at Fort Bowie. Military and civilian travel began to dramatically decrease with the building of the railroad across Arizona in the 1880s, as the railroad right of way curved north of the Dos Cabezas and Chiricahua Mountains two miles from the old station at Dragoon Spring, through the new town of Willcox, to Bowie and San Simon and its exit from Arizona at Stein's Pass. Aside from its use by the military, travel through Apache Pass became desultory, largely local traffic between the San Simon and Sulphur Springs Valley.

Its usefulness in Indian campaigns ended, Fort Bowie was ordered decommissioned, and on October 17, 1894, the last troops marched away. Local residents moved in and stripped the post of lumber and anything else of value, and the property was sold to a rancher. Gradually the old post fell into ruin, and Apache Pass lost its importance and became a place of comparative solitude for the first time in hundreds of years. Still occasional travelers used the old trail, and Apache Spring continued to pour out its waters as it has for time unknown.

There have been more changes, and for the better since that long-ago time. The old stage and wagon road, though it follows the Butterfield Route only a short distance, is graded and maintained now through Apache Pass. The National Park Service has re-acquired the site of Fort Bowie and has stabilized the remains. From a parking lot, a one-and-one-half-mile trail leads to the old fort, where courteous rangers keep watch. Along the trail are the ruins of the old Butterfield stagecoach station, the post cemetery, the battlefield where Cochise and Mangas contended with the soldiers in the Battle of Apache Pass, and Apache Spring, still patiently pouring forth its calm waters. In places, the old stagecoach route can actually be seen. There are markers at the scenes of wagon train massacres and other bloody engagements, and grave markers.

Most of all, at last in Apache Pass is peace, quiet and solitude. The spirits of the men, white and red, who contended for it so proudly and courageously are forever at rest.

Fifteen miles east of Benson on I-10 take the Dragoon exit to the town. Take dirt road south 2½ mi. to the Jordan Canyon Rd., turn left 1 1/10 mi. The old station is to the left across the wash plainly visible from the road. The cemetery is a few feet left of the station. Please do not disturb anything at this historic site. It is on forest service land; the service preserves it.

Apache Spring in Apache Pass. Vital to the Apaches and to the travelers on the Butterfield trail, the Battle of Apache Pass for possession of it was fought in 1862. The spring still flows the year around.

CHAPTER 3
Dragoon Spring

By what means the Dragoon Mountains of southeastern Arizona came by that picturesque name does not seem to be recorded anywhere. Neither, it seems, is the time when the mountains were first referred to by that name. There is basis for an educated guess at the answers, however. Doubtless the Apache Indians who inhabited them, and the Spanish and Mexican governments who once exercised nominal political control over them, had names for them. They became American territory with the Gadsden purchase of 1853. Rand McNally's 1879 map of Arizona shows them as an extension of the Galiuro Mountains to the north, but the military map of the same year gives their name as the Dragoon Mountains.

The word "dragoon" itself is rooted in Europe and refers to military units composed of heavily-armed mounted troops. Units of the United States cavalry that carried heavy carbines as well as the usual cavalry weapons, sabers and revolvers, were known as "Dragoons." Such a unit was the Third Cavalry, which is said to have been stationed in the mountains. Again the exact location of their station is obscure, but it was probably at Dragoon Spring on the north slope of the mountains, discovered by scouts of the Third in 1856. Reference to the previously unnamed mountains and spring as "Dragoons" from then on would only be natural.

Water has always been a precious commodity in the arid southwest. The wild and fierce Chiricahua Apache Indians made these mountains, the Chiricahua Mountains to the east and the Sierra Madres in Old Mexico to the south, with the valleys between and large areas surrounding them, their homeland. The Indians intimately knew every spring and seep in those mountains and heavily depended on them, as the streams in the valleys were shallow and had a disconcerting habit of drying up or running underground in dry seasons. The Apaches had used Dragoon Spring for hundreds of years. The stronghold of their great chief, Cochise, in 1856 probably in his thirties and at the height of his physical powers and prestige among his people, was only a few miles to the south of the spring in the Dragoon Mountains.

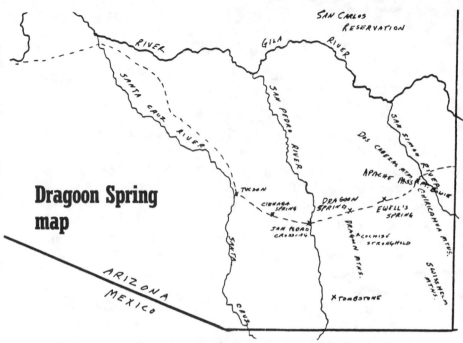

Dragoon Spring map

It is probable that travelers through Apache country had known of Dragoon Spring before its discovery by the cavalry. Traffic through the region increased as a southern route was sought to California after the discovery of the gold fields there in 1849, and travelers too had to have water. When the Butterfield Overland route was laid out from St. Louis to San Francisco in 1857, its stations were built where water was available at surface streams and springs; wells were dug where no other water was available. Dragoon Spring and Apache Spring in the Chiricahua Mountains forty miles to the east, both in the heart of land of the Chiricahua Apaches, were sources vital to Butterfield stations.

For a time the Apaches were not a problem. Cochise was at peace with the Americans, whom he regarded as allies of a sort against the Apaches' traditional enemies, the Mexicans. Traffic on the emigrant trail moved and used the waterholes in comparative safety. Butterfield agents made agreements with Cochise and furnished him with goods, his people were paid for furnishing the stations with firewood. The stations themselves were discreetly built a half-mile to a mile from the springs, thereby avoiding constant direct contact with the Indians when they watered at the springs. It was not until January 1861, when a tragic error in judgment by a young lieutenant in dealing with

Ruins of the Dragoon Spring Station on the Butterfield route. In upper left and upper right are outlines of rooms. Room at left was the station office, where Silas St. John fought for his life.

Cochise upset this delicately mutual arrangement, and sent the Chiricahua Apaches on an implacable warfare against the Americans that lasted until September 1872.

When the Butterfield Overland was laying out its route in 1857, then, the first five stations from Arizona Territory's eastern border were on the San Simon River, in Apache Pass at Apache Spring, south of the Dos Cabezas Mountains near Ewell's Spring, on the north slope of the Dragoon Mountains at Dragoon Spring, and on the west bank of the San Pedro River. Work crews trekked westerly along the trail, building stations as they went, leaving agents and station personnel to put on the finishing touches. In August 1858, a crew arrived at Dragoon Spring to construct the station. Of the ten stations built of rock along the line as fortresses against Indian attack, this was the most westerly. The solid walls of rough mountain rock laid together with clay were 45 feet by 55 feet, ten feet high. There was one gate, just inside of which an eight-foot square office was walled off with an iron safe built into the wall. In the opposite corner a store room of the same size was walled off. Half of the enclosure was the living quarters, the other half was the stock corral, to keep the Indians from rustling the animals.

Forest Service sign identifies rock-walled ruins of Dragoon Spring Station on the Butterfield route, approximately three miles from present-day Dragoon.

Late in August the construction crew moved on to build the San Pedro Station, leaving Butterfield agent Silas St. John with three other company men and three Mexican laborers to roof the station and man it. With St. John were the line's blacksmith, James Hughes of New York, James Laing of Kentucky, and William Cunningham of Iowa. The Mexican laborers were Guadaloupe and Pablo "El Chino" Ramirez of Sonora and Bonifacio Mirando of Chihuahua.

The night of September 8th, 1858, Laing stood the first watch. At midnight Silas posted Guadaloupe Ramirez to take the second watch. St. John slept in the office, Cunningham in the store room, Laing in the center room with the stock, Hughes and the two laborers outside. An hour later St. John was aroused by the uneasy stirring of the stock, then wakened by the sounds of blows and outcries. He leaped from his bedroll but was unable to grab his rifle from its scabbard attached to the saddle he was using for a pillow before he was set upon by the three Mexican laborers, who were attacking the Americans. They were armed with a chopping axe, a broad axe and a sledge hammer.

St. John fought them off with his bare fists, trying to get his rifle out of the scabbard. He averted a blow at his head, took an axe gash in his hip, knocked down Mirando, and took a gash in the palm of his hand. He got a gash in his forearm as he was jerking the rifle out, swinging it like a club to ward off his attackers, but took a blow with an axe that severed his left arm below the shoulder. Unable to raise the rifle to fire it, he swung it so viciously as to drive the men from the room. He dropped the rifle to seize a pistol, and when the gun fell the Mexicans attacked him again. He managed to fire a shot from the pistol, at which the Mexicans dropped their weapons and fled.

Even so, St. John's situation was indeed grim. He managed to get a tourniquet of a handkerchief and stick around his severed arm and stop the flow of blood. He could not stop the bleeding from the axe wound in his hip. He dragged himself around to his three companions, some of whose moans he could hear. Hughes was dead outside, his skull crushed by the sledge hammer. Laing was alive and conscious though his brains could be seen through a gash in his skull. There were three deep gashes in the skull of Cunningham, who moaned continually for water. There was no water in the station. The mules, terrified by the smell of blood, reared and plunged frantically.

Unable to drag himself the half-mile to the spring for water, St. John made it to the top of a stack of sacked grain. There he watched for the Mexicans to return or for Indians to attack. All day Thursday he watched, wracked by thirst and swatting at clouds of insects. When night came St. John drove skulking coyotes away from Hughes' body with pistol shots, and at midnight Cunningham died. The next day was the same. Bodies of the dead were attacked by ravens and buzzards, St. John was in and out of a stupor. That night packs of wolves approached, fighting among themselves and howling ghoulishly. On Saturday the ravens and buzzards returned, and by Saturday night St. John had fallen into a coma.

On Sunday morning, four days after the station crew was attacked, a correspondent of the Memphis *Avalanch*, named Archibald, approached the station from the west with a guide, traveling to El Paso. They hesitated when no flag was seen flying, nor any activity about the station, but soon discovered the horrifying situation. While Archibald hurried to the spring for water his companion tried to do what he could for St. John. As Archibald returned from the spring a road building crew with three wagons, in which were Col. James B. Leach and Maj. N. H. Hutton, arrived traveling westward. They revived St. John and dressed his wounds. Hughes and Cunningham were buried in the same grave. On Monday, Laing died and was buried beside them.

Two riders were sent to Fort Buchanan, forty miles south of Tucson, for a doctor. A direct route was considered unsafe, so they made the trip through Tucson. They reached Fort Buchanan on Wednesday. The assistant surgeon, Dr. B. J. D. Irwin, left immediately with an escort. The surgeon rode sixty miles through hostile Indian country, arriving on Friday. He cleanly amputated St. John's severed left arm, his ministrations saving the man's life. Six days later St. John was moved to the hospital at the fort, and three weeks later he rode a horse to Tucson and went back on the job, a recovery so remarkable that it was noted in medical journals. St. John, only twenty-three years old at the time, lived a long and useful life in Arizona and died at eighty-four. The three Mexican murderers escaped across the border and were never caught, though the company had offered a large reward for their capture.

In 1861 the Civil War broke out, Butterfield ceased operations, and the station at Dragoon Spring was abandoned for a time.

The spring and station still naturally were a camping place on the emigrant trail, because of the necessity for water. In May 1862, the two hundred Texans under Captain Sherod Hunter who had occupied Tucson for the Confederacy retired eastward toward El Paso in the face of the numerically superior Union force, the California Column under General James H. Carleton, advancing from the west. On May 5th while camped at Dragoon Spring the Confederate soldiers were attacked by the Chiricahua Apaches. Four of Hunter's men were killed, thirty-five mules and twenty horses were run off by the Indians. More graves were added to the cemetery at Dragoon Spring Station.

Two months later the California Column moved eastward from Tucson toward New Mexico. It came under constant harrassment by the Chiricahua Apaches under Cochise, no respecter of the color of uniforms, who attempted to waylay stragglers and drive off stock. John Jones, a dispatch carrier, was attacked by the Apaches, and though Jones outran them his guide named Chavez and his escort, one Sgt. Wheeling, were killed. On July 14th the Column's advance force was camped at

Stone-covered graves in cemetery at Dragoon Spring Stagecoach Station. Buried here are personnel of the Butterfield stage line killed by Mexican laborers building the station, and soldiers slain in fights with the Apaches.

Dragoon Spring. Part of it entered Apache Pass on July 15th to secure Apache Spring for the main force, leaving the supply wagons at Dragoon Spring. At Apache Spring on the 15th the Battle of Apache Pass was fought, and on the 16th the rest of the advance force moved up from Dragoon Spring to Apache Spring and another battle with the Apaches. More graves were added at Dragoon Spring.

Despite the establishment of Fort Bowie by Carleton in Apache Pass, movement through southern Arizona was desultory except in force during the Civil War because of the depredations of the thoroughly aroused Cochise and his rampaging warriors. In his memoirs, Arizona pioneer Billy Fourr tells of traveling across the old trail in 1862 with a large party, seeing Arizona for the first time, and of a beautiful sunset viewed from Dragoon Pass. Near this spot he would one day establish a ranch where he would spend the last sixty years of his life. In 1862, however, fires were spotted further up Dragoon Canyon that were Apache campfires, and the traveling party lingered no longer than necessary.

After the Civil War the military posts were re-established, the soldiers came back to them, and attempts were made to bring the Indians under control. The long, bloody process, marked with excesses and cruelty on both sides, took twenty years. Other stagecoach and freight lines were established, and emigrant trains traveled the old trail. The station at Dragoon Spring sprang to life in service to them all once again. It was the mail delivery point for comparatively nearby ranches, and small settlements such as Russellville, near a mine a short distance to the north.

In 1872 a peace treaty was finally made with Cochise, and for a time there was a measure of rest from the depredations of the Chiricahua Apaches. The peace treaty provided a reservation for the tribe taking in the Dragoon and Chiricahua mountain ranges, the Sulphur Springs Valley between them, and parts of the San Simon Valley to the east and the San Pedro Valley to the west. A white friend of Cochise, a military scout and cattleman named Tom Jeffords, was the Indian agent. Together they kept the peace during Cochise's lifetime.

It was not easy to do. Bred to the warlike ways of their ancestors, Apaches did not take easily to reservation life. They traveled at will across the border to Old Mexico, raiding and plundering their traditional enemy as they always had. In 1876 Cochise died and his son Taza became the tribal chief. Though Taza worked closely with Jeffords and tried to keep the peace himself, he was never as strong as his father had been. War chiefs such as Geronimo, Juh, and Natchez, another son of Cochise, gradually gained in power. White men were jealous of the extent of the reservation, which they coveted. Incidents increased on both sides, and the Bureau of Indian Affairs began looking for an excuse to abolish the reservation and send the Chiricahua Apaches to San Carlos.

The Bureau found it at Dragoon Spring. Two white traders named Rogers and Spence had set up shop in the old Dragoon Spring stage station, where among other things they sold whiskey made of wood alcohol, laced with cayenne and tobacco. When the Chiricahua Apaches went on a hunt in the Dragoon Mountains in the spring of 1876, their camp broke out in a violent quarrel that was further inflamed by the traders' whiskey. Jeffords sent word to the traders demanding that they stop selling whiskey to the Indians, who when denied more then murdered the two traders. The killers were named Piarhel and Pionsenay, who also murdered two of his sisters, then took a party of Apaches on a raid of the settlers in the San Pedro River valley. Twenty-eight troopers under a Lt. Hendley from Fort Bowie took up the Indians' trail, but failed to catch them.

Jeffords then asked Natchez, son of Cochise, to bring in the murderers. Natchez turned the job over to his younger brother, Tarjay. Jeffords was under orders to cooperate with plans to remove the Chiricahua Apaches to the San Carlos Reservation preparatory to closing the Chiricahua Reservation. Knowing this, the Chiricahua Apaches held a council on June 4th with Taza and Natchez arguing for cooperation with Jeffords and some of the war chiefs rebelling. A fight broke out in which Piarhel was killed and Piosenay shot through the lungs, Tarjay's father-in-law Esquinay and three other Apaches who had tried to defend them were killed, and Taza was wounded. Soldiers arrived from Fort Bowie and ended the bloodshed. On June 12, Taza and most of the Chiricahua Apaches were removed to San Carlos. The Chiricahua Reservation and Dragoon Spring were restored to the public domain.

In the years 1878 to 1881, the Southern Pacific Railroad was building its line across Arizona, closely following the old emigant trail, but with some deviations. Building through Dragoon Pass, the railroad bypassed the Dragoon Spring stage station two miles to the north. It continued northeasterly around the north side of the Dos Cabezas Mountains, avoiding Apache Pass, no longer needing the waters of the springs.

In 1886, Col. J. F. Stone, for whom Stone Avenue in Tucson was named, operated a gold mine at a peak called Helen's Dome within sight of Fort Bowie in Apache Pass. On October 6th he started for Tucson with a gold shipment in a chartered stagecoach. In the party were a friend, Mr. Kahler, a miner named Hinton, a driver and a shotgun guard, and four troopers escorting the coach. Approaching Dragoon Pass the little group found that Apaches were trailing them. They stopped and hid the gold. No one knows the number of Apaches that pursued them, but apparently Stone tried to make a run for the old Dragoon Spring station and whatever protection it might afford.

The Stone party did not make it. A fourth-of-a-mile east of the station they made their stand. After a terrific battle they were all killed, and the bodies were stripped and mutilated. No cache of gold was ever found despite a hundred years of searching and may still be hidden somewhere on their trail. Legend has it that there was a hidden cave somewhere near the spring, the location of which has been forgotten. It is improbable that any in Stone's party knew of the cave, or had time to cache the gold there if he did.

Southern Arizona was shaken with an earthquake in 1887, and from that time Dragoon Spring stopped flowing. No longer would its life-giving waters sustain the men, white or red, that had vied for it so fiercely. No longer was it needed by the ox, mule and horse; the tracks of cattle and deer leading to it faded away. There is serenity, now, peace and quiet on the north slope of the Dragoon Mountains at the spring and the station. The Forest Service has preserved for us the ruins of the old station and the remains of its rock walls. Still outlined are the rooms where St. John fought for his life and his companions murdered by the Mexican laborers. In the little graveyard are stone-covered mounds, beneath which sleep forever the valiant station crew and the men of Hunter's and Carleton's commands slain by the Apaches. Signs erected nearby commemorate them, and the old

Butterfield trail can be faintly discerned trailing off into the chaparral.

A couple of miles to the north a roadway crosses the steel rails at Dragoon Summit on the Southern Pacific Line, where Wyatt Earp as a federal marshal stopped the train in 1882 and searched it for, but failed to find, an outlaw named Hank Swilling implicated in the killing of Wyatt's brother. Three miles farther north is an interstate freeway bearing thousands of travelers every day. Few, if any, would have more than a passing interest in the old spring, trail and station almost within their sight and the travail of those who preceded them a hundred years ago.

MAP TO REACH
DRAGOON STATION RUIN

Fifteen miles east of Benson on I-10 take the Dragoon exit to the town. Take dirt road south 2½ mi. to the Jordan Canyon Rd., turn left 1 1/10 mi. The old station is to the left across the wash plainly visible from the road. The cemetery is a few feet left of the station. Please do not disturb anything at this historic site. It is on forest service land; the service preserves it.

Old buildings and, at left, U.S. post office in Dragoon, Arizona, 1987. The Southern Pacific rail line is just out of the picture to the left, and approximately three miles away in the hills to the right is the site of the Dragoon Spring Station.

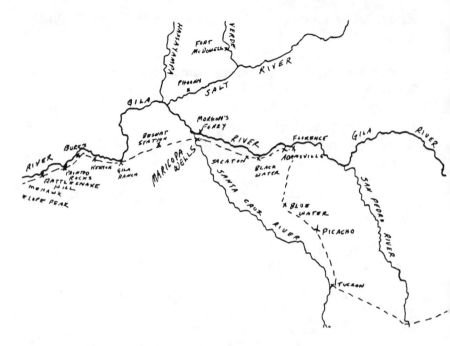

Maps for Chapter 4 - Maricopa Wells

Maricopa Wells Station site is on the Gila River Indian Reservation south of Phoenix. Little remains of it, and it is difficult to locate. Just south of the Maricopa highway bridge a trail, almost certainly the remains of the old Butterfield trail, rounds Pima Butte and goes into the desert. There are many tracks diverting from it, and it crosses deep washes. About three and a half miles west a trail inter-sects the Southern Pacific Pipeline right-of-way. From where the pipeline makes an elbow to a more northwesterly direction, the station site is approximately 7/10 mile west. An easier route would be driving the pipeline main-tenance road from Maricopa northward to the elbow. The pipeline road is a private easement, it must be remembered. The sketch is not drawn to scale.

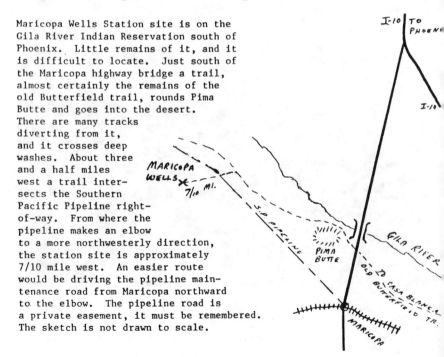

CHAPTER 4
Maricopa Wells

In the desert on the Gila River Indian Reservation, about fifteen miles south of the great metropolis of Phoenix, eight miles north of the hamlet of Maricopa, and four miles west of the Phoenix-Maricopa highway are a few low mounds of earth. They are what is left of adobe walls melted back into the earth from which they came. Nearby are several round holes in the ground, which once were wells, but now are empty, caved-in, dry and dusty. Few people know where it is or ever visit it with the possible exception of cowboys, some Pima and Maricopa Indians, and now and then a few curious travelers to remote spots in the Old West. Yet little over a hundred years ago it was the most important location in Arizona Territory. It was on the mind and on the tongue of every traveler through central Arizona, for everyone passing through whether it be north and south or east and west eagerly sought it. It was the principal crossroads of Arizona Territory, and its name was Maricopa Wells.

They sought it for its life-sustaining waters, an oasis in the vast Arizona desert, the only habitation of white men for hundreds of miles around. There were only two other villages in the huge, empty primitive territory, the pueblo of Tucson to the south and the new capital of Prescott far to the north. The primitive trail between them ran through Maricopa Wells. The southern overland route from the states to the east and California to the west followed the Gila River across the desert as the only dependable source of water, and it ran through Maricopa Wells. This rutted, wandering, dusty trail, forerunner of continent-spanning railroads and interstate freeways, took weary months to travel on foot, or in animal-drawn vehicles.

The earliest records of travel across Arizona Territory mention Maricopa Wells, identified by the surface pools of water to be found there. It was a short distance from the year-round flowing Gila River, near the Santa Cruz River said to flow underground for long distances, and the point where the long Vekol Wash joins the Santa Cruz and the Gila. In this low spot the ground was tight from a centuries-old deposit of silt, the water table was high from ages of unpumped ground saturation, and pools of water stood on the ground. The water was once described as "so strongly impregnated with alkali that the porous earthen jars into which it was put. . . were incrusted on the outside with a solid white deposit of soda and potash, but it was the best to be had in many miles and, bad as it was, was always a welcome beverage to thirsty souls choked with the impalpable dust of the traveled roads. . ." From the descriptions in their journals, the exploring priests, Father Eusebio Kino in 1694 and Father Francisco Garces in 1775, had rested from their journeys at the waters of Maricopa Wells.

When the Mormon Battalion under Col. Philip St. George Cooke crossed Arizona in 1846, it camped at Maricopa Wells in the month of December. Cooke's men deepened some of the water pools, and dug several wells while there. When the overland trail became choked with traffic with the gold rush to California beginning in 1849, the wells became of great importance to travelers, who had to load up with enough water to carry them and their animals through the trip across the dreaded Forty-Mile Desert to Gila Ranch on the river's great bend to the west. By taking this forty-mile "short-cut" across the desert, they avoided having to follow the Gila around the north end of the Sierra Estrella, a hundred miles out of their way.

In 1857, the San Antonio and San Diego mail route was established between Texas and California, and Maricopa Wells was established as its exchange point. Here the eastbound carriers met the westbound to exchange mail. The only facilities were a rude shelter and make-shift corral of brush. Two years later the Butterfield Overland route carrying mail and passengers from St. Louis to San Francisco began service over the southern route, and Maricopa Wells became an important station on the line. The Butterfield company erected several adobe buildings and stout corrals. There were at least half-a-dozen good, deep wells, and the friendly Pima and Maricopa Indians helped improve the primitive conditions by furnishing food from their farms, and hay for the stock. When the Civil War broke out in 1861, however, the Butterfield line ceased operations and never started up again. For a time, the sparse facilities at Maricopa Wells fell into disuse, though traffic over the Gila trail continued to grow even during the war years.

A colorful pioneer merchant, John B. (Pie) Allen, well-known and respected in southern Arizona, was the next to take over at Maricopa Wells. In later years Mr. Allen became known for being the first on the scene at new mining camps to establish a general store, such as he did at Gunsight, Allen's Camp near Quijotoa, and even in Tombstone itself, where the famous Allen Street was named for him. In 1864, he settled at Maricopa Wells where he repaired and improved the buildings and corrals abandoned by Butterfield, and built new and larger facilities for his station. He ran a trading post and carried on a large trade with Indians on the nearby reservation and with travelers along the Gila River trail.

In 1867, Allen sold his interests at Maricopa Wells to the George F. Hooper Company of what was then Arizona City but is now Yuma. The Hooper company was rich and influential, and established still better facilities at Maricopa Wells for a growing traffic, not only over the east-west Gila trail to California, but the north-south route from Tucson, the new capital, and southern Arizona points to the original territorial capital at Prescott and the numerous mining camps springing up to the north. Maricopa Wells was also the terminal on the supply route for Fort McDowell, which had been built in 1865 some distance to the northeast on the Verde River. The station at Maricopa Wells, then and for the next twelve years to be the cross-roads of central Arizona, was now heavily stocked and the focal point of travel and trade.

The station and facilities at Maricopa Wells were purchased from Hooper in 1870 by Mr. James A. Moore and his partner, Larkin W. Carr, and for the next eight years Maricopa Wells was at the peak of its prominence and prestige. It was at the center of the Tucson-Yuma section of the Kerens and Mitchell stagecoach line operating across southern Arizona, and here Mr. Moore, superintendent of the stagecoach line, made his headquarters. The year 1870 also saw the beginning of the settlement of Phoenix fifteen miles to the north on the bank of the Salt River, and a road was quickly established from it to Maricopa Wells. The road from Phoenix passed by Henry Morgan's trading post near the Pima Village of Sacate (not to be confused with Sacaton), crossed the Gila on Morgan's Ferry, and intersected the overland trail.

An eyewitness account of the station and the people who inhabited it were given in his memoirs by Mr. Emerson Oliver Stratton, a widely-respected pioneer who began his Arizona career as the bookkeeper at Maricopa Wells. "When I arrived at Maricopa Wells," recounted Mr. Stratton, "I found a typical stage station consisting of one building only, but a whole town in itself. The rambling adobe structure, one room in width, ran around three sides of a great hollow square enclosing about two acres, in the middle of which was a huge stack of wild hay. A high adobe wall completed the fourth side. In the center of the wall were large wooden gates for teams, and a smaller door in one of the gates for people.

"All the rooms, except the office and the store, opened only into the square. The office, the store, the saloon and the living quarters faced the road. One side of the building contained the stables and blacksmith shop. Running down the opposite side was the hotel—meals a dollar per. The standard meal at a stage station—whether breakfast, dinner or supper—consisted of black coffee, red beans, bacon and biscuits. At Maricopa Wells we were more fortunate. We had a man, a herder and butcher in one, who kept fifty head of cattle and supplied the hotel and the store with fresh meat in the winter and dried beef or jerky in the summer. And once in a while a sack of onions or potatoes would arrive from San Diego."

According to Mr. Stratton, also living at the station were James A. Moore and his family consisting of a wife, young twin daughters, a son named Arthur and a step-son, John Crampton, who also left his reminiscences written in later years, a telegrapher named Taylor, teamster John Boutou, blacksmith William Trout, line rider and apprentice telegrapher Miles Gearhart, a man named Carter in charge of stage horses, the herder and butcher, a Mexican roustabout, a Chinese cook, an Indian laborer named Santiago with his wife Tonica and their infant, and several stage drivers, among them Milt Ward and Hank Thompson. Their nearest neighbor was Henry Morgan at his trading post and ferry on the Phoenix and Fort McDowell road, four miles distant.

"Though small, " continued Mr. Stratton, "Maricopa Wells was a busy place. The stages passing twice a day, one eastbound and one westbound, changed animals and fed their passengers here. When troops were discharged, and this was often, the stages were full both ways. At other times there was a predominance of passengers from the west...Californians coming into the country...and easterners who had gone by train or around the Horn to San Francisco, then...into Arizona by stage. Then, too, Maricopa Wells was the division point for Phoenix, Fort Verde and points north.

"The camping ground outside the enclosure was also a busy place. Great freight trains of three or four wagons and eight to twenty mules were often camped there, and detachments of soldiers, from a few scouts to one or more companies, might turn in for the night. Soldiers scouting through the immediate country made Maricopa Wells their supply station, and all westbound traffic, whether or not they camped, had to load up with enough water to last across the desert...to Gila Bend.

"In the center of the camping ground was a well with an odd history...One day there came along an old drunken fellow much in need of the cup that cheers. He declared that he could not drink the muddy, brackish water from the river, and offered to find good water in exchange for a bottle of whiskey. He dug the well in front of the station and hit fine, pure water. The well was a deep one, and the water was raised by a team of mules or oxen at the end of a long rope."

In addition to the bustle in the campground, along the trail, stagecoaches arriving and leaving, very important people to be

Maricopa Wells Station in October 1874. Outside telegraph office (from left) the telegrapher Sergeant Miles Gearhart, station proprietor James A. Moore, man behind pole unidentified, line rider Billy Baxter, bookkeeper Charles H. Naylor, stage driver Milt Ward. In far background is hat of J. Arthur Moore, son of James A. Moore. At right is the Papago Indian cart driver and handyman Santiago. At lower left is his wife, Tonica, holding their infant. Identified by John F. Crampton, Moore's stepson. (Courtesy Arizona Historical Society)

entertained, and maintenance of every kind of vehicle, Maricopa Wells station carried on a large volume of commerce. There was the trading post general store, the saloon, and barter with the Indians who brought in wheat and traded it for beans, sugar, cloth and other items. A large volume of business with the government had to be handled with due regard for red tape restrictions. Arriving and departing mail had to be sorted and properly routed. When the first telegraph line through southern Arizona was built in 1873, Maricopa Wells was a principal station. The telegrapher had to be on duty to shunt the lines in the direction that messages flowed. Two soldiers, apprentice telegraphers and line riders, were always stationed there. The frequency of the poles, sixteen to the mile, was insufficient, so the wire was also borne by tall saguaros and mesquite trees.

Surviving accounts of Maricopa Wells by those who journeyed there naturally vary in their assessment of it. The log of one young army officer, reprinted in the "Journal of the U.S. Cavalry Association," in 1889, said: "As we came in the early morning down the slope to the 'Wells,' after an all-night march across the desert...our eyes were gladdened by the sight of a verdant spot which, to our weary souls, promised a pleasant rest; but a nearer approach proved it to be an illusion as deceptive as the mirage of the desert. The green turf of our imagination was only a scanty growth of salt grass, each blade of which was strong enough to stand alone, and so rank with alkalai that even a hungry mule could not eat it and live.

"Maricopa Wells...was the only place between Fort Yuma and Tucson where the table fare ever rose above the sodden, greasy level of bacon and beans. Owned by the only firm of any importance in the southern part of the territory, and controlling nearly all of the government contracts and freighting business, they had their trains always on the road and in this way could supply themselves and their friends with all the necessaries and some of the luxuries of life--including the best brands of whiskey and champagne to be obtained in San Francisco. It was a veritable oasis in the desert..."

One of a series of letters from another army officer, reprinted in the *Journal of the West*, gave this description: "Arriving at Maricopa Wells station (from which I write)...we are camped on the alkali grass, and got a miserable supper from Mr. Moore who keeps the station. On our arrival, his wife and daughters were absent, having gone to a miners' ball at the Salt River settlement. They reached home a little later and were not an uncomely looking household. A crowd of greasy, savage-looking Indians, of both sexes and all ages, are lounging around the store, which is under the same roof with the dwelling house. Mrs. Moore has given us a very graphic account of the ball at Salt River which, no doubt, in the estimation of the unrefined and grotesque participants, was magnificent. They danced on a dirt floor, and it was very dusty. This...proved to be a very good substitute for snuff, and produced a very pleasing sensation upon the sensitive membrane of the nasal organs. We are told there is but one board floor in Arizona, and that is in the house of the Governor.

"The daughters of Mrs. Moore look quite gay and lovely, dressed as they are, a la mode Arizona, not unlike the variegated wraps noticed on some of the Indian women. They are full of merriment and rather loud talking, but withal not very uncouthly mannered...In the store are two Indian girls dressed in large, dirty chemises, with faces ornamented by black lines drawn down from the eyes and mouth. They wanted pinoche—that is some cakes made from dust-colored flour and very dark brown Mexican sugar. I bought a couple of pound pieces and gave to them, which they immediately tucked under their chemises without acknowledging the gift. In the entry between the store and dwelling hang large pieces of fresh beef on lines stretched in the yard, large quantities of the same article to be sun-dried or 'jerked.' The post office is a small room opening out of the store, where we found some old numbers of *Harper's Bazaar* and the *Los Angeles Weekly Star*, which can truly be regarded as the pioneers of literature and civilization in this wild country..."

The Moore family to whom the above made reference was one of the best-known and liked in the entire territory. Situated as they were at the territory's crossroads, they met every traveler whether of high or low station, and frequently entertained some of the most famous. James Armor Moore, frequently alluded to as "Captain Moore," had acquired that title as a whaling captain who reached San Bernardino, California, by way of San Francisco and the California gold fields. He ran a butcher shop in San Bernardino, where he met and married Matilda Jane Barrett Crampton, of whom more will be said later. She had a son, John Crampton, by a previous marriage. James Moore came to Arizona to work at the Vulture Mine near Wickenburg, but when Fort McDowell opened in 1865 he went to work there running the sutler's store for the Hooper company.

In 1867, Camp Reno was established in the Tonto Basin, and Moore opened a store there for Hooper. Not long afterward he and a partner, Larkin Carr, bought the McDowell and Reno stores from Hooper, and ran them until 1869 when they sold them to William B. Hellings, around whose flour mill near what is now Papago Park in east Phoenix the settlement grew that became the city of Phoenix. The following year Moore and Carr bought the station at Maricopa Wells. Both Moore and Carr were fine, honest men, highly regarded throughout the territory.

Mrs. Moore as Matilda Jane Barrett had come from Missouri in a covered wagon over the Gila trail to California, in the same wagon train with the ill-fated Oatman family. While

Tombstone of Henry B. Harriman, "died at Sweetwater, Arizona, July 15, 1877, aged 40 years and 5 months," lies flat, broken into four pieces. Harriman died of smallpox.

some of the wagons in the train rested at the Pima villages Royse Oatman had pressed ahead alone. Most of the family was murdered by raiding Apache Indians on the trail, and the boy, Lorenzo, left for dead. Lorenzo revived when the Indians had left and started back along the trail, where he was found and rescued by the following emigrant families of which the Barretts were one. She bore Moore a son, who was called Arthur, and the twin daughters, Susan and Clara. The children were very young while at Maricopa Wells, except for the stepson, John Crampton, who was in charge of the station's stock and was a general handyman. The twins were famous throughout the territory, attended a finishing school in San Francisco owned by a sister of the celebrated Arizona pioneer Charles D. Poston, and later married men who became famous and prominent in the territory.

Moore bought out Carr's interest in Maricopa Wells in 1874 and remained there until 1878 when it became apparent that the railroad would bypass the station. He then sold it to Barnett and Block, and went to work for a number of years at the Silver King mine near the present town of Superior. He became ill and went to California for treatment, but died there in 1883. His widow, his son Arthur and John Crampton moved to Globe, where they lived for a long time as highly-respected and well-known citizens of Arizona territory.

The memoirs of another respected and long-lived pioneer, Charles M. "Charlie" Clark, in the *Arizona Republic* on April 10, 1929, included a colorful account of life at Maricopa Wells station and an affectionate remembrance of Mrs. Moore, who was known as "Aunt Jane from San Berdoo" and her husband as "Uncle Jimmie." Clark was the first telegrapher at Maricopa Wells. "Because of Uncle Jimmie's forced absence on business," wrote Clark, "the management of affairs at the home station fell upon the shoulders of "Aunt Jane," a manager of prompt decision and superlative efficiency.

The blacksmith and wheelwright repair shops for the line were located at the home station, and the men employed in these departments, with the men gathering wild hay and wood, and the various stage drivers who laid over at the end of the division, numbered perhaps thirty men. They were paid a monthly wage which included their board, and for the purpose of feeding this crew a kitchen and large dining room were provided. Many an old timer ate in that dining room when passing through... This dining room was about thirty feet long and only wide enough to permit the Chinese cook to pass behind the benches upon which the diners sat.

The room was of adobe finished inside. The roof was made of poles upon which rushes were laid, the whole being covered with about a foot of adobe dirt. There was no ceiling, nor floor, the latter being the original dirt when the building was laid out. This dirt floor was sprinkled by the Chinaman after each meal, and thus kept in good, hard condition. The table which extended the full length of the room was covered with a well-worn oilcloth of vintage of 1864, and carried the scars of successive swabbings on the part of the various Chinese cooks who had presided in the kitchen since it was installed--crushed, cracked and darkened by use and abuse to a dull black.

The help, who were furnished their 'grub' as part of their monthly remuneration, were allotted their respective seats and required to occupy the same seat on all occasions. Suspended above the table, by swinging bows of iron hinged to the rafters, were successive loops of faded, dirty calico, bolt width, dropping to within ten or twelve inches from the top of the table. These bows were fastened together to move in unison, and were controlled by a half-inch rope attached to the bow at the foot of the table and extending through a hole in the adobe wall to the yard in the rear, where it was supposed to be operated by a Pima Indian pulling it back and forth. Punkah? I don't know, but it was all of the first syllable with some to spare.

The idea was to keep the flies in motion while the guests were eating, which it did NOT do. These same flies had learned to recognize the battering of the big steel drill bar which the Chinese notified the world to 'come and get it.' By the time the paying boarders arrived, the flies to the 'steenth' generation were 'on the job and working steady.' At the upper end of the table, in contrast to that portion occupied by the help, about four feet of the surface was covered by a white cloth. The service was silver and porcelain, the cups and saucers were thin. There were fresh biscuits, honey, ham and plenty of eggs for breakfast and fresh beef for dinner, green vegetables from Salt River ranches, a large pitcher of real milk, and the menu and ensemble were a bit homelike. Down the line the bread was dark, the bacon or side of meat often carried yellow streaks and was strong, the Arbuckle brand coffee was boiled to a density black as tar. The sugar, when there was any, was dark brown, the beans, cabbage and spuds were strictly 'hunter's style,' and the difference between the family mess and the grub of the hired hands was noticeably great.

When I reached 'the Wells' and applied to 'Aunt Jane' for board, she took me into the dining room and about half-way down the help end of the table showed me a place on the bench, which she said would be my regular seat, or as she put it, 'yours permanent. Your board will be $45 per month just the same as the two repairmen who work for you.' These two repairmen were soldiers assigned to my station as repairmen, and for instruction as soldier operators.

Clark's memoirs went on to say that, after a few days of this, he seated himself at the "family's" end of the table one morning and gorged on ham and eggs. He was promptly 'called on the carpet' by "Aunt Jane," who told him to stay in his place at the table or eat elsewhere. Clark chose to eat elsewhere. He obtained a cookstove, bought supplies from the government commissary and from the Indians, and learned to cook from Henry Morgan at Morgan's Ferry, for whom he brought in wood and washed the dishes for a month in exchange for lessons. He became so good at cooking that eventually he became an expert pie-maker. He recalled, "One day I made a batch of apple pies that come out extra nice...I slipped one on a plate, covered it with a napkin, and gave it to one of my repairmen to take over to "Aunt Jane" with my compliments. He returned shortly saying, 'The old woman smelled the pie and weakened. She said to me, 'Tell him thankye, and I'll return the plate when I eat the pie.'

That evening after sundown arrayed in a white Marseilles dress with ribbons flying, "Aunt Jane" came over to my house carrying my pie plate and napkin, and seating herself in one of two rocking chairs which I had purchased, said, 'Clark, that there pie was rale good. I didn't know you could cook that-a-way. The girls and me are going to have chicken dinner tomorrow, and we would like you to come over.' Just like that. Not a word about my rank impertinence to her right in her own house, and from that day we were good friends to the day of her death in Globe eighteen years later. Unlettered, uncouth perhaps, but certainly enjoying to the extreme the courage of her convictions and unafraid to act upon them.

A character known familiarly throughout the Southwest, ...I witnessed her on one occasion swinging an axe by the end of the handle chase a big Missourian out of her corral, and then throw his shotgun after him. I once heard her tell A. P. K. Safford, then Governor of Arizona, that he would have to lay over at the 'Wells' until an empty seat came along, as two soldiers had that day come over from Fort McDowell with government transportation, which was cash, while he was riding deadhead. Many an old-timer, prospector, stage driver or tramp remembered 'Aunt Jane' with gratitude. No hungry man was ever turned from her door. She lived hard and worked hard, depriving herself that her children might be sent 'inside' to secure the education she had been denied. Having successfully raised and educated her children, 'Uncle Jimmie' having preceded her by two years, she laid down her burden in Globe about the year 1890, a good mother, a good friend, a square fighting enemy, a typical frontier woman of pioneer days in Arizona. May she rest in peace.

Mr. Clark was hazy in his dates, as Mr. Moore died in 1883, and Mrs. Moore passed away in 1899.

Additional reminiscences of what day-to-day life was like at Maricopa Wells were provided by the memoirs of Mr. Stratton and Mr. Crampton. Mr. Stratton:

Some people believe that it was the Indians who made life unsafe in these faraway places. It was, in the very early days when the Indians were bad all over Arizona, and again in later days when the Apaches kept the stations around and east of Tucson in a state of great suspense. But in my time at Maricopa Wells our greatest danger was from Mexicans and renegades from Mexico. It was easy to make a raid across the line, then sneak back to the Mexican side and lay the blame on the Indians. . . While some of the Mexicans in the area were bad, most of them were hard-working, law abiding people.

Our roustabout at Maricopa Wells was such a one. He taught me a few things in short time I knew him. . . Mr. Moore instructed me to have the roustabout cut and stack a quantity of (native) hay in the corral. . . For several days I looked around for implements with which to cut hay, but could find nothing but a pitchfork. I finally confided in the Mexican, and he nodded his head, 'Si, si.' In a few minutes he came back with the pitchfork and a stout, sharp hoe. . . Then I learned that the best clumps of grass grew in the rocky ground around trees whose leaves and dead branches through the years had fertilized the immediate soil. For this reason the hoe was the most practical cutter.

On another occasion I asked the Mexican to haul in some wood. One of the best firewoods is dry mesquite, and in those days there were large areas of dead mesquite all over southern Arizona. In seasons of heavy rain the old dry lake beds and charcos would fill up, and water would stand around the base of the mesquite trees for several days. The torrid heat of the sun would then scald the bark just at the water's edge, and in time the wood would become very dry and brittle but never rotten. I was much surprised when the Mexican took a sledge hammer with him to gather wood, instead of an axe. Then I learned that it was almost impossible to cut the stuff with an axe, but it broke readily.

Mr. John Crampton, stepson of Mr. Moore, outlived his mother by some forty years and left several interesting manuscripts and letters concerning Maricopa Wells and the stage line between Tucson and Yuma. As self-styled "handy-Andy," he traveled it frequently doing maintenance and trouble-shooting. Every month or six weeks he and the blacksmith at Maricopa Wells would load up a spring wagon and visit the stations shoeing horses. The blacksmith made up the shoes in advance, and Crampton would straighten and point the nails, which then came unfinished in hundred-pound kegs from the factory. Crampton was also in charge of furnishing stock, horses and mules to the various stations.

The stations on the line were approximately those of the old Butterfield Overland route, but varied somewhat, particularly to the east where it went to new communities that had sprung up. Mr. Crampton named them westward from Maricopa Wells as Desert Well in the middle of the Forty-Mile Desert, Gila Ranch at the bend of the Gila River, then Kenyon's Station, Burk's Station, Stanwick's Station, Painted Rocks (which were actually petroglyphs), Rattlesnake Hill, Mohawk Station, Antelope Peak, Mission Camp, Filibuster Camp, Gila City, Yuma. From Maricopa Wells east the stations were Casa Blanca, Sweetwater, Sacaton, Montezuma, Blackwater, these first five at trading posts on the Pima Indian reservation, Adamsville, Florence, Wheat Wells, Picacho Station, Desert Wells, Bailey Wells, Nine-Mile Water Hole and Tucson. Reflected here are the new towns of Florence which still exists and Adamsville which does not, a station kept by a man named Wheat, and one at a ranch owned by Bailey.

Wrote Mr. Crampton: "It took five days and five nights in those days for the stage to go from Tucson to San Diego. The fare was $90 cash. Greenbacks were worth only sixty to sixty-cents on the dollar and nearly everything was paid in gold or silver. Meals at the stage station were a dollar... The coaches traveled about five miles per hour. That was schedule time. It took three days and three nights to go from Yuma to San Diego. The coaches would lose one to two hours at each station where they changed horses. The wagon would be greased, meals would be prepared for six to eight men and the horses changed." Of interest in this vein is the rate schedule for passenger service announced in the Tucson *Arizona Citizen* of May 13, 1876: From Tucson to Florence, $8; to Maricopa Wells, $18; to Phoenix, $20; to Wickenburg, $30; to Prescott, $40; to Yuma, $40; to San Diego, $50; to San Francisco, $65. The rate on express baggage was thirty-five cents per pound.

Except for one of those historical caprices that shape the destinies of men and nations Maricopa Wells might today be an Arizona city. That caprice was the decision by the builders of the railroad across southern Arizona not to lay its tracks to Maricopa Wells. Instead, the railroad by-passed it eight miles to the south. In a short time it would replace all travel and transportation drawn by animals, the ox-cart, the covered wagon, the freight wagon and stagecoach. James Moore saw it coming and sold the station at Maricopa Wells in 1878. In May 1879, the railroad established a way station by its tracks which it merely called 'Maricopa.' Gradually the steel ribbons crept across Arizona until in 1881 they linked with those building west on some yucca-covered flat in New Mexico. At its Maricopa way station plans for a new town were being made, and lots were being sold. At the station at Maricopa Wells the new owners held on, losing business every day.

In 1887, the railroad built a spur line through Tempe into Phoenix, and tied the spur into its tracks five miles east of its Maricopa way station. That created a new 'Maricopa' which immediately sprang up at the intersection of the Phoenix spur. The old way station was deserted at once as everyone picked up and moved to the new. Though a new trunk line was built through Phoenix and Tempe forty years later, the hamlet of Maricopa still exists, the center for a vast region of cotton farms. The Phoenix spur line around which it began was itself eventually torn up and the roadbed abandoned.

For Maricopa Wells the building of the spur line by-passing it to Phoenix was the final dagger through its lifeline. No one stopped there now on the road to or from Phoenix to the railroad, no stagecoach or freight wagon was necessary. The post office and telegraph station were moved to the new town on the railroad. By 1889 Maricopa Wells was completely abandoned and the once-thriving and bustling community became a fading memory. The dirt and pole roofs of the buildings collapsed, the adobe walls washed away again. Mesquite and palo verde trees grew up in the old corrals, the wells dried up and collapsed as the underground water was pumped out and the table lowered. The reason for its existence was gone. But it will never be forgotten, so long as the courage and perseverance of pioneers building a new life in the Old West are cherished in the hearts of men.

CHAPTER 5

Morgan's Ferry

In Arizona Territory two of its three great rivers, the Salt and the Gila, (the third being the Colorado), flowed all the year around from east to west across the land. Near its center they met, the waters of the Salt flowing into the Gila in its westward course. They were not yet tamed by dams upstream, winding placidly through mountains and across deserts in dry years, wild and fierce at flood stage. Two pioneer men, both widely known and respected throughout the territory in their day, operated ferries across these rivers near Phoenix. Their names were Charles Hayden and Henry Morgan, and fate and history dealt with them in starkly contrasting ways.

Hayden established his ferry across the Salt ten miles east of Phoenix in 1870, brought his bride Sally to his station where she became its charming and vivacious hostess, fathered the famed Senator Carl Hayden, and built a flour mill near his ferry where the community that grew up around them evolved into the city of Tempe. Morgan operated his ferry across the Gila River fifteen miles south of Phoenix, built a trading post near it, lived there with an Indian woman in a common law marriage, left no heirs, and because of unalterable forces in the march of progress his ferry and the community of Maricopa Wells near it were passed by and eventually completely abandoned. Charles Hayden's name still lives in the memory of Arizona the state, while Henry Morgan's has slipped into time's misty oblivion.

The inseparable stories of Henry Morgan and Morgan's Ferry are still to be found in the archives of the Arizona Historical Society and the Arizona Historical Foundation, the reminiscences of his contemporaries and the files of the newspapers of his time. Born in Wisconsin in 1841, Morgan arrived in Arizona in 1864. He had a contract with White and Noyes of San Francisco to erect a steam flour mill at the Pima Indian village of Casa Blanca, where the Pimas were raising large quantities of a superior strain of Sonoran wheat. Despite the staggering job of getting the machinery over primitive trails from San Francisco and erecting the mill with primitive labor, Morgan got the job done, and stayed for about a year. Doubtless this mill replaced the one owned by trader Ammi

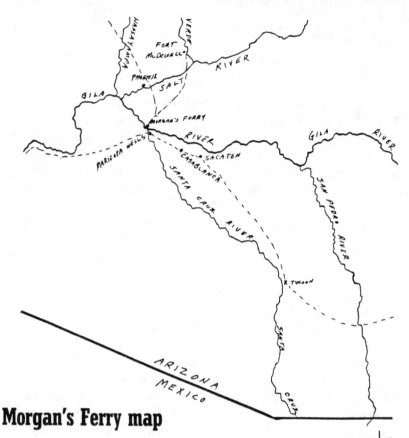

Morgan's Ferry map

All traces of Morgan's Ferry have disappeared,
washed away by periodic floods by the Gila
River. Since the highway to Maricopa Junction
was authorized to be built by way of Morgan's
Ferry, it may be assumed to have stood where
the highway bridge now crosses the Gila. A
station was located on both north and south
banks, the trading post probably on the south
bank nearest the Pima Village of Sacate close by.
The military supply trail to Fort McDowell passed
here from its terminus at Maricopa Wells four
miles to the west. The Butterfield Overland
trail passed nearby, about a mile to the south,
as it rounded Pima Butte on its way to Maricopa
Wells. The Maricopa Junction to Phoenix railroad spur ran on the west side of the highway.
It was torn up and the roadbed leveled long ago.
The piers of the railroad bridge stood in the
riverbed until the mid-1980's, when another
flood on the Gila wiped out the highway and its
bridge for weeks. Then the riverbed was chan-
nelized at this point and the old piers removed,
the last vestiges of the spur line.

White, who had operated a mill, store and stagecoach station in Casa Blanca, but had sold the mill to the Bichard brothers who moved it to Adamsville.

Though he was only twenty-three years old, Morgan and the Pima Indians, the first he had ever seen, developed a mutual affection. Except for one bitter incident, for many years thereafter he was their spokesman and arbiter with other white men, particularly government representatives. He learned their language, lived with them, treated them kindly and fairly, and even fought with them and their neighbors, the Maricopa Indians, in their battles with raiding tribes. In his memoirs, Mr. John F. Crampton of Maricopa Wells station recalled a great battle fought in the mesquite thicket in front of the station between the Pimas and Maricopas on one side, and the marauding Yumas on the others. The Pimas and Maricopas were aided by some white men, one of whom was Henry Morgan, because of whose generalship the Yumas were soundly beaten and routed.

These battles were fought mostly with war clubs and sometimes lasted for days. After this one the field was left littered with bodies of the dead of both sides. A letter from a young army officer to the *Los Angeles Star* in 1872, published in the Journal of the U.S. Cavalry Association, described his visit to the field of such a battle fought a year or two before, a mile or two west of Maricopa Wells. "The Maricopas," he wrote, "were the remnants of a once large tribe which had nearly been annihilated in a battle with the Yumas and Cocopahs. The whitened bones of the slaughtered Maricopas and their opponents that lay, piled upon the field when I visited it, showed how desperate and destructive the struggle had been. Since their disastrous defeat, the tribe had virtually placed themselves under the protection of the Pimas..."

In 1864, Arizona was a wild, savage, unknown wasteland. It had been a separate territory only one year, and had only two villages. One was the sleepy, Mexican pueblo of Tucson to the south; the other was the new state capital, Prescott, being built on Granite Creek protected by Fort Whipple to the north. Phoenix was not even a faint thought in anyone's mind. But in 1864, Henry Wickenburg discovered the Vulture gold mine eighty miles north of the Pima Reservation. There in 1865 went Henry Morgan to build the quartz mill for Chase and Company, to work the Chase extension of the Vulture Mine. He stayed two years.

In 1867, Morgan returned to the land of the Pimas and Maricopas, and built his station that was known thereafter as Morgan's Ferry. It was on the banks of the Gila ten miles west of Casa Blanca, about four miles east of Maricopa Wells station, then the third most important habitation in Arizona. All traces of Morgan's Ferry and station have disappeared. However, it was on the south bank of the river at about the location of the bridge on the Phoenix–Maricopa highway. It was on the road to Fort McDowell from its supply trail terminal at Maricopa Wells, near the Pima village of Sacate (not to be confused with Sacaton, fifteen miles east). Only one map shows the ferry's location, the military map of 1879. There are references to a road authorized by the Maricopa County supervisors in 1877 to be built between Phoenix and Maricopa Wells by way of Morgan's Ferry.

Doubtless the station at Morgan's Ferry was like all the others in the primitive land, on the Gila plain barren of any building material except earth and a few palo verde and mesquite trees. The walls were of sun–dried adobe bricks mortared with mud, the roof ocotillo poles or mesquite limbs cross–laid and covered with arrowweed, the roof a thick layer of adobe mud. The floor was of hard–packed caliche clay, watered and swept daily to keep it hard. Probably as time went on the buildings and furnishings improved, but not very much. It is certain that floods washed the ferry away more than once, and it had to be rebuilt. Here Morgan labored at ferrying and trading with the Indians for twenty–five years, wearing out four stoutly–built ferry boats in the process.

Some descriptions of Morgan by his peers survive. Charlie Clark, first telegrapher at Maricopa Wells, described Morgan as a "gruff, uncouth fellow who it was reported had been a pirate in the Gulf of California years before. He was rough, blasphemous to a degree, but a fairly good fellow when he was not drunk. As a result of some fight he had been in, he claimed to have seven bullets in his body, three of these being plainly visible just under the skin, one under his right breast and two just beneath his shoulder blades, a record that he was evidently 'taking 'em a–goin'." Historian James M. Barney described him as "a man of few words and sometimes decided opinions, but had a kindly personality and was amiable and friendly with those he liked." John F. Crampton tells of his having a Pima Indian wife.

Morgan himself described the Pimas with whom he had such close ties as being then sober, honest, upright and fair in all their dealings, and with ideas of justice that balanced the affairs of life to the most delicate scale. They had one fault, and that was a minimum opinion of the commercial integrity of women. When they found Morgan selling goods to their squaws on credit, they laughed at him. Morgan always succeeded in getting his money, however. The Pimas always paid their bills when the crops were good, and when the crops failed for a season the village chief came to the rescue with a guarantee that was always made good.

Before 1870, according to the memoirs of Phoenix pioneer Madison Loring, Morgan formed a partnership with Daniel Dietrich under the name of H. Morgan and Co. to conduct the trading post at Morgan's Ferry, and they soon branched out into the new town of Phoenix beginning fifteen miles to the north. The *Arizona Miner* on September 15, 1872, said "H. Morgan & Co. have finished their new building on Washington Street, joining onto a new building of John George so as to form but one structure. A piazza extends along the whole front built entirely of sawed lumber, neat and tasty in appearance, and, with the trees in front, their rich green foliage forming a natural curtain, it is a pleasant place in which to loaf." It was on the north side of East Washington between Center and First Streets, a portion of the ground afterward occupied by the Woolworth company. On June 28, 1879, the **Phoenix Herald** reported that "Morgan and Co. are erecting a large frame building on Washington Street opposite Meyer's stable. Part of it will be used as a grain warehouse."

For some time Morgan and his business enterprises prospered. The newspapers of the time carried advertisements praising the quality and variety of the company's merchandise and its good service. One of the company's advertisements read "H. Morgan and Company, Washington Street, Phoenix, and Morgan's Station on the Gila River, Importers and Dealers in groceries, clothing, dry goods, liquors, tobacco and cigars, etc., at prices to suit the times." Interesting was an item in the *Herald* on April 20, 1878: "Oswald Link, Wm. Holland, Henry Morgan, John P. Clum, and Robert Eccleston transfer all their right, title and interest in the Morgan ditch to the Morgan Ditch Company;

consideration $1 and certificates of stock." Two years later Clum would establish the most famous newspaper in the territory, the **Tombstone Epitaph,** and in 1881 would become mayor of that storied city. He was a last–minute replacement on the election ticket, and the man he replaced was Eccleston.

The newspapers also carried stories revealing Morgan's combative nature. He was fined three hundred dollars for "fooling with a sixshooter too seriously for the bodily comfort of his adversary." He opposed the candidacy of Phoenix pioneer George Mowry for sheriff, and said so in a slanderous newspaper advertisement. In a few days he ran another advertisement of retraction, probably to escape Mowry's wrath in court. In 1879, "considerable excitement was occasioned by H. Morgan entering Salari's Restaurant, drawing his revolver and endeavoring to shoot P. Dolan. He was only prevented by bystanders wrestling his revolver from him. In the melee he was injured so severely as to necessitate his remaining in bed today."

Newspapers also carried the account of Morgan's killing a Mexican at his station on the Gila on August 21, 1879. Morgan surrendered to authorities, and was arraigned for the slaying of Jesus Figorro. Defended by attorneys J. T. Alsap and A. C. Baker, "the evidence so fully justified Mr. Morgan in the act that the Justice discharged him from custody at once." No circumstances of this shooting were given, but since in pioneer days holdups were a common hazard of station keepers at lonely outposts, some inferences may be drawn.

Tragedy struck H. Morgan and Company on July 13, 1880, when Morgan's partner, Dan Dietrich, was shot and killed by Pima Indians at their station on the Gila River. According to accounts, Dietrich was alone, and had locked the store at sundown. He was standing about six feet away from it, when he was shot four times in the back and fell forward on his face. His body was found by Henry Morgan the next morning. Morgan testified at the coroner's inquest that when he found Dietrich's body there were about twenty Indians off to one side about thirty feet. Morgan carried the body into the station, then discovered tracks coming from and returning to the river. He testified that the only one he thought likely to murder Dietrich was a long–haired Papago with whom Dietrich had a quarrel a year previously. The Papago lived below the station, but did not trade there, as Morgan would not allow him on the premises.

The coroner's jury found that Dietrich was killed by a person or persons unknown, and Morgan offered a reward of three hundred dollars for the arrest and conviction of the murderer. The *Phoenix Herald* on July 30, 1880, referred to the "capture of one of the murderers" of Dan Dietrich, but there is no other reference to this murder. This single one was made in the context of an account of a brutal assault on Henry Morgan himself, in which he was left for dead but recovered.

The account carried by the *Herald* was as follows:

David Hickey, an eye witness, said...he was attending the lower station...About three o'clock yesterday afternoon Morgan and Tom Rogers arrived from Phoenix. After a few minutes rest Morgan told Hickey to saddle his horse, as he wanted to go and see the Indian chief (who lives a few hundred yards distant). Mr. Morgan went to the Indian camp, saw the chief, and told him to get up behind and return to his house, as he wanted to talk to him, which the chief did...Morgan told the chief he had heard that he had given Dietrich's murderer a horse to escape on. On hearing this, the chief hollered to some of his warriors, who came running up, overtaking them before reaching the house. The chief took his knife and threatened to cut Mr. Morgan, but doing no damage. Mr. Morgan...told him he meant them no harm, and they soon quieted and left.

About an hour afterward Dave Hickey, who was outside, saw about one hundred Indians coming toward the station, and, running inside, told Mr. Morgan who ordered the doors and windows closed and barred. The Indians soon arrived and demanded admittance, saying they wanted Morgan. The men inside then armed themselves and waited. The Indians soon broke in the door, and a number of them rushed in and dragged Morgan outside. The Indians were not afraid of the firearms, and the white men did not shoot. Outside, Morgan was knocked down with a large mesquite club, three feet long, hit three times, and was, no doubt, supposed to be dead by the Indians. With the second blow the club was broken off two feet from the handle, and the last blow about a foot from the handle. They said they were only after Morgan and would not hurt the others.

Hickey saddled his horse, intending to come to town, but they said he should not until the next day. He then told them he wanted to go to Harris' station, about half-a-mile away, to get something for Morgan's head. This they consented to. On reaching Harris' he left the road, intending to circle around to the east, regain the road and come to Phoenix. They soon saw him, and took after him. Then followed an exciting race.

He, having the swiftest horse, kept out of their reach, but they followed him to Broadway's ranch, ten miles, which he made in less than an hour. He was soon in town, and a party of six, including Dr. Conyers, were soon on their way back. On their arrival at the station they found everything quiet, Tom Rogers attending Mr. Morgan. They returned to town bringing Mr. Morgan, who now lies in his room back of the store, having sufferred a severe fracture of the skull. He is attended by Drs. Jones and Conyers, and is doing well, though badly used up...

On August 20, 1880, the *Territorial Expositor* of Phoenix reported that "yesterday Dr. Conyers performed a very neat surgical operation in removing from the head of Mr. Henry Morgan...two pieces of the skull, one of them being one–and–seven–eighths–inches long by three–fourths of an inch wide. Notwithstanding this operation, Mr. Morgan is able to walk around and enter into conversation with no apparent effort or pain." So from this fearful beating at the hands of the Pimas he had befriended and with whom he had traded so long Morgan recovered, but from that time on his fortunes declined for the remainder of his life.

The following June, Henry Morgan was back doing business at his station on the Gila. On August 26th it was reported that a flood on the river had washed his ferry away, but four days later he was again running in first–class order, crossing and recrossing teams. An ad placed by Morgan in the *Phoenix Herald* on August 31st said, "Attention Teamsters! On and after this date I will be prepared to do ferrying to any extent at my old ferry on the Gila. By the new road recently opened up from Maricopa to Phoenix, via my ferry, teamsters will experience no trouble in making through trips at any time or season." Notice the reference to "Maricopa" rather than "Maricopa Wells." An historic event had taken place. The railroad had been built across southern Arizona in 1878 and 1879. It had bypassed the established stagecoach station at Maricopa Wells by eight miles to the south. A new terminal called "Maricopa" had been established on the railroad, and Maricopa Wells was doomed. In a short time it was completely abandoned. Freight moved through to Prescott from Maricopa for three cents a pound, or two–and–one–half–cents from Morgan's Ferry. It would be a few years until the railroad built a spur line into Phoenix; then Morgan's Ferry would be doomed.

Newspaper notices late in 1881 and 1882 told of the decline of H. Morgan & Co. "The business house of H. Morgan & Co. in this city was closed by the sheriff this morning and attachment for the sum of $5,800.08 in favor of A. Weil, a San Francisco creditor of the house. We hope the difficulty will be only temporary." "Sheriff Orme is having the goods, wares and merchandise of H. Morgan and Co. sold at public auction to satisfy the judgment of A. Weil. . . Billy Blankenship is attending to the auctioneering."

"The Sheriff this morning sold the real estate of Morgan and Co. The store, building and lot, etc., were bought by Irvine and Co. for $2,060. The house and lots on West Washington Street were bought by E. Thompson for $1,210." "The Morgan property on Washington Street, adjoining the Capitol Building, recently sold on execution, has been redeemed and was Monday purchased by Pierpont Miner." "The Morgan property opposite Monihan's stables on Washington Street was redeemed yesterday and sold by H. Morgan to J. L. B. Alexander. The consideration was $2,250."

His business ventures in Phoenix having failed and his partner gone, Morgan retreated to his trading post and ferry on the Gila. Apparently he mended his relations with the Pimas and business prospered there once again. He lost another friend in 1884, a one-time sheriff of Elko County, Nevada, Lloyd Hill. Hill had gone to Morgan's Ferry to visit for a few days, but early in June started out to walk back to Phoenix. Morgan may not have known that Hill had started out walking, for he became alarmed for Hill's safety and sent an Indian after him with a horse. It was too late. Hill had lost his way and perished from the heat.

References to Morgan and the ferry and trading post through the rest of the 1880s and early 1890s were only to the effect that Morgan was well and business was good. Small wonder, with Phoenix and other communities to the north, free at last of the fear of Apache raids, growing and prospering. Morgan was on the only north-south road through central Arizona, and his ferry had a monopoly on all traffic crossing the river. That all ended when in 1887 the railroad built a spur line into a growing Phoenix. The line was built from Maricopa, making a bridge across the Gila River necessary. It probably was within sight of Morgan's Ferry.

The spur line itself ran along the west side of the Phoenix–Maricopa highway. It was torn up and the roadbed leveled again long ago. Piers of the old railroad bridge stood for a hundred years and could be seen by motorists crossing the Gila on the highway bridge. Morgan's Ferry would eventually be doomed, though not necessarily the trading post. The Phoenix

Herald even stated as late as April 1, 1891, that "the Salt and Gila River ferrymen are said to be coining money these days." There seems to be no reference to how long Morgan remained before giving up his station. But his friendship with and knowledge of the Pima Indians and his ability to speak their language with all its dialects then stood well with him. He became an interpereter and expert on Pima Indian affairs with government authorities, receiving up to twenty dollars a day for his services, and representing others who needed an agent with the tribe.

The Pimas were fond of a sort of native hooch called 'tiswin,' which they fermented from the fruit of the saguaro cactus. The government forbade the making of this brew, but the Pimas paid no attention, simply hiding the knowledge from the authorities when the tiswin barrel was bubbling. When it was ready, the tribe would retire to a remote spot on the reservation and put on a smashing party, sometimes lasting several days. The big danger was that the fiery drink allowed savage instincts to rise to the surface, and then there were always fights and inevitably killings. The Indians always tried to keep these deaths from the authorities with their version of "mum's the word." Henry Morgan was often enlisted by law enforcement agencies to help them find the killer.

In 1891, Morgan noticed that Pimas from the Salt River Reservation that had recently been established east of Phoenix had been conspicuously absent from town for several days. He concluded that the Indians were off on a tiswin spree, and when next he met one of the Salt River Pimas he asked if the party was on. The Indian replied that it was a thing of the past. "How many were killed?" inquired Morgan. The answer was that, though drunkenness was general, nobody had been murdered. There was something in the Indian's manner that aroused Morgan's suspicions, however, so when he met another member of the Salt River Pimas, he changed tactics. "Is that Indian that got shot at the feast dead?" he asked. "No, but he can't live long," replied the Indian.

Another such killing took place in 1892, which came to light in an almost casual way. An Indian boy whose father was in jail came in to Phoenix from the Salt River Reservation to visit. As a bit of neighborhood gossip he told his father the news. The conversation was overheard by Henry Morgan, who questioned the boy and found out the details of the incident. During a howling tiswin drunk one Chonah was stabbed by De–Ne–A–Doc. Chonah's soul took flight, and so did De–Ne–A–Doc. Armed with a warrant for the murderer's arrest, Morgan and a Marshal DeNure set out for the reservation believing that De–Ne–A–Doc would not stay away very long.

Late the next day Morgan and DeNure returned to town, what they found causing them to abandon the job. After the killing, De–Ne–A–Doc had fled the reservation, but was so loaded with tiswin that he had to lie down to sleep it off. When Chonah's friends had recovered sufficiently from their bout with the liquor, they set out on De–Ne–A–Doc's trail and found him in his drunken stupor. Chonah's friends forthwith lynched his murderer with thoroughness and dispatch. So many Indians had been involved in the affair that Morgan and DeNure gave up trying to sort out the details and those involved, feeling that justice had somehow prevailed.

The *Arizona Republican* of October 14, 1893, carried the following story: "A horrible murder was committed on the Pima Reservation at the Gila Crossing, fifteen miles below the city, last Friday night. It was the crowning episode of a three–day tiswin drunk in which that department of the tribe had been engaged. The victim was Rosa, the belle of the reservation, said to have been the handsomest squaw in the territory. The instrument used was a club and the woman's head and face were beaten into a shapeless mass.

The first word of the murder was brought to town the next morning by some Maricopas who were questioned about it closely by Henry Morgan, but they pretended to know only that a murder had been committed, by whom they were unable to say though it was plain they knew more than they were willing to tell. They said that a deputation of Indians had gone to Sacaton to report the affair to the agent.

"Mr. Morgan laid the matter before the district attorney and Sheriff Murphy. Since then he has been collecting information from other Indians who have come in from the reservation. Although they speak of the affair with great reluctance, Mr. Morgan has gathered that the murder was committed by the woman's husband whose name he has not been able to learn. The feast was one of the most furious ever celebrated on that reservation, a circumstance due to the fact the tiswin was produced from the grape, rather than from the milder saguaro.

In 1899 Morgan arranged for some Pimas to appear at a carnival in Tucson. Some two hundred Indians participated in a parade, but the women refused to ride, as they never rode astride a horse in public. Morgan even stated that during the days he had kept his station on the Gila, they would hitch their horses on the farthest outpost and walk in. The arrangements made by Morgan, reported to have been entirely satisfactory to the Pima chiefs, was fifty cents for those appearing in the parade, food for themselves and feed for their horses for one day, and one dollar a day for archers who were to be employed for three or four days.

With the years after the turn of the century Morgan's physical condition began to deteriorate and his mind gave way. At a sanity hearing in December 1905, it was revealed that "he had been living in a small shack near the electric light plant" for a number of years. Mr. Seth Byers, who instituted the hearing, and others had looked after his wants, but now he was hallucinating, and it was thought best to place him in an asylum. To this he was committed, and there he died on October 15, 1908 at the age of 67, and was buried in the Pioneer's Cemetery in Phoenix.

Henry Morgan's epitaph, while not carved on his tombstone, continues to live in the history of early Phoenix. It was brought to light in a magazine, the *Arizona Graphic*, on March 24, 1900. A pioneer jubilee was to be held, and old residents who had moved away had been invited back for the gathering. One of the very first residents of Phoenix but by 1900 living in Scranton, Pennsylvania, was Mr. Madison F. Larkin. Mr. Larkin wrote to the *Graphic*, inquiring about several old friends including Henry Morgan, and "Count Darrell Duppa, the great epitaph writer, one of which I will quote. It was not necessary for a man to be dead in those days for Darrell to write his epitaph, which accounts for its having been written for Henry Morgan:

Weep! Phoenix, weep! and well you may,
Great Morgan's soul has passed away.
Howl! Pimas, howl! Shed tears of blood,
And squaws, bedeck your heads with mud.
Around his grave career and canter,
And grieve the loss of beads and manta.
His head so large endowed by fate,
No hat could fit but number eight.
He died as leaves of autumn fall
And dying said, "I've fooled you all."

CHAPTER 6
Oatman Flat

Near the western edge of Maricopa County, Arizona, on the old Gila trail is the scene of one of Arizona's countless pioneer tragedies. Seventy bee–line miles, one hundred covered wagon miles, and a hundred and thirty years in history removed from Phoenix, and now almost abandoned, it is known as Oatman Flat. It was only another sandy flat spot between the sluggish Gila River flowing just north of it and the rough ridges of volcanic rocks just south of it until the historic incident that named it. Later on it was a station on the Gila trail when that was the bustling overland route from the populous east to California. The old station on the sandy flat lived for many years, until the building of the railroad across southern Arizona doomed the Gila trail, forcing it and its colorful stations into historical obscurity.

Arizona's own celebrated historian, Sharlot Hall, in an article for a magazine in 1909, told the tragic story of the Oatman family, for whom the flat was named. It began in Independence, Missouri. The father, Royse Oatman, was a native of Vermont, and his wife of western New York. They had arrived in Missouri by way of Pennsylvania and Illinois. They were members of a religious sect called Brewsterites, which had broken away from and been excommunicated by the Mormons. Their leader, James Collins Brewster, preached that the prophesies of Esdras told of the land of Bashan which was at the mouth of the Colorado River. Bashan would be the refuge of the godly from His wrath which was surely coming. At Fulton, Missouri, Royse Oatman sold his farm and with the others of his faith traveled with his family to Independence to join the westward movement to Bashan. The family was his wife Mary Ann, and seven children, Lucy who was seventeen; Lorenzo, a lad of fourteen; Olive Ann, thirteen; Mary Ann, seven; and Royse, Jr., C. A., and a baby brother.

The wagon train pulled out of Independence on August 9, 1850. All of the party was well–supplied with wagons, cattle, household goods, and carried what was thought to be provisions for several months, as well as goods for barter with Indians later on for more food supplies. Travel was pleasant during the

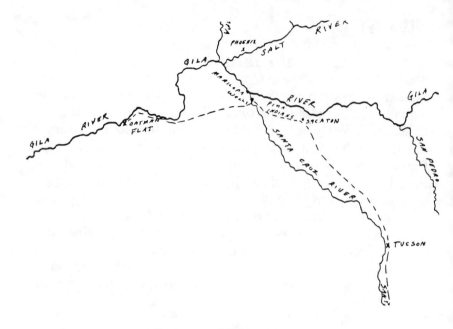

Oatman Flat map

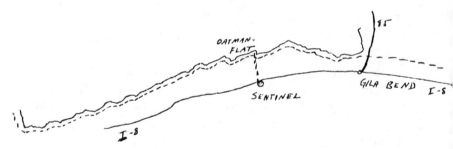

This sketch is not drawn to scale and is
intended to show only the route in relation
to other features. There is no established
road to Oatman Flat, only desert trails with
no road signs. Inquire locally at Sentinel.
From Sentinel to Oatman Flat is approximately
ten miles. A pick-up truck or four-wheel drive
vehicle is recommended, as are other precautions
due because of the time of the year, etc.

summer and fall over the Santa Fe Trail, but divisions arose within the company that came to a head at Las Vegas, New Mexico. Some wanted to continue to the Colorado River, some wanted to settle in the Rio Grande Valley, others were for going on to the California gold fields. The party split, some continuing westward toward California, the rest veering southward on the Cooke Wagon Road, laid out by the Mormon Battalion under Col. Philip St. George Cooke in 1846. Royse Oatman was the leader of the southerly-traveling division, the smaller of the two.

Indians had already stolen part of the wagon train's horses and mules, and more such thefts and sparse graze soon left the Oatman party short of draft animals. Slower travel due to the weakened stock reduced the food stores, and the travelers found it difficult to buy more from the Mexicans and Indians. These people were themselves short of food supplies because of a year of severe drought. More and more the dream of a settlement on the Colorado faded and the travelers decided to continue to California by way of Tucson and Fort Yuma to settle. Then, while camped to rest their stock and do some hunting to replenish the food supply, the Apaches stole twenty more head of stock, and it became necessary to abandon some of the wagons and goods.

Following the San Pedro River south, the wagon train came to Santa Cruz in Mexico on Christmas Day, 1850. Traveling back northward along the Santa Cruz River, they came to Tubac in January. All of the horses had now been lost or stolen, most of the cattle killed for food, and cows were now hitched to many of the wagons in place of the lost oxen. At Tubac the inhabitants begged them to stay for at least a year to help them stave off Apache depredations, offering them farm lands as an inducement. The Oatman party thought itself to be too small to be of much help, and was anxious to press on, and so it did. At Tucson again they were offered lands to farm if they would stay, and the wagon train rested itself and its animals for two months. Some of the families decided to remain in Tucson for a year, but Royse Oatman and two of the others decided to continue to the Pima villages on the Gila River, hoping they could trade some more of their household goods to the Pimas for corn, wheat and mesquite beans. The drought had also hit the Pimas hard, and they had no food to sell, barely enough to keep themselves alive. Their warriors also warned that the Apaches were very active,

Ruins of the ranch home and stagecoach station built by Wm. H. Fourr in 1864 at Oatman Flat. (Courtesy Arizona Historical Society)

and urged the travelers to return to Tucson until the route was safer.

At Maricopa Wells the Oatman party met Dr. John LeConte, a famous entomologist who was coming from California eastward and told them that he had met no hostile Indians. This and his dwindling supplies caused Oatman to decide to press onward to California, where he had relatives. The other two families decided to stay a while longer at the Pima villages, but on March 11, 1851, Royse Oatman with his family and two wagons headed westward now alone along the Gila trail. It was a sad parting from their friends, and Mrs. Oatman was very reluctant to press on with her small children, but into the wilderness of sand and greasewood they went, cows now pulling the wagons in place of the oxen they no longer had.

They traveled so slowly that Dr. LeConte, traveling with his Indian guide, overtook them camped on the Gila River when he was returning to California. He was alarmed at their condition, and saw that they would never make it to Fort Yuma without help. Dr. LeConte took with him a letter from Royse Oatman to the post commander at Fort Yuma, Major Samuel P. Heintzelman, asking him for aid in the form of food and draft animals. However, thirty miles further on the horses on which Dr. LeConte and his guide had been traveling were stolen by Yuma Indians, forcing the doctor and his guide to travel on foot and therefore much more slowly.

Before hastening on to Fort Yuma with all possible speed, Dr. LeConte, left a message on a card fastened to a tree stump warning Royse Oatman of the danger. Though it could never be proved, the surviving children believed that their father found this message, but concealed it from the family to keep them from more worry. Fate was fast closing in on them now. They missed the trail, their animals became exhausted from pulling wagons through the deep sand, and the family spent the night camped on a small island in the Gila River. During the night a fierce sandstrom struck. The following downpour of rain drenched them and everything they had. It is not difficult to picture the mother huddled with her children in one of the wagons trying some way to keep dry and warm, and the father and his oldest son trying to keep the canvas from blowing away, the wagons from toppling over, and the cows from bolting in the ferocity of the storm.

During the night the storm spent itself, and the exhausted animals managed to drag the wagons from the island to the riverbank. They were too weak to pull them up the bank to the sandy flat above it, so everything had to be unloaded and carried up by hand, then all of the cattle hitched to each wagon which was pulled and pushed one at a time up the riverbank. It was March 18, 1851, and the remainder of the day was spent drying their possessions and reloading the wagons, in preparation for travel the next day. Late in the afternoon they were having their evening meal of bread and beans when one of the children, some accounts say it was Lorenzo and some Olive, alerted the family to the approach of a band of Indians.

Royse Oatman assured his family there was nothing to fear, though it was apparent to them that he himself was greatly agitated and alarmed. The Indians, about fifteen Yavapais armed with clubs, lances, crude knives and some with bows and arrows, rode into the Oatman's camp. Surly and insolent, they asked at first for tobacco, and Oatman gave them all he had. Then they asked for bread, and were given some. When they demanded more, Royse Oatman explained that there was no more, that their supplies were very low, and that he had sent to Fort Yuma for supplies and draft animals. The Indians withdrew a short distance and conferred among themselves, while the Oatman family nervously continued their wagon loading.

Suddenly the Indians attacked the family with war clubs. The father was killed first, then the mother (now pregnant again) as she tried to protect her children. The baby was run through with a lance. Lorenzo, the boy, was brained with a club and his body thrown over a rocky ledge. Except for two of the girls, Olive and Mary Ann, the heads of every member of the family were smashed with war clubs as the horror–stricken girls watched. The Indians rifled the wagons, even stripping the shoes from the dead bodies and taking those of the girls. They were driven off into captivity, forced to walk barefoot as the Indians drove them and the cattle across the river, across the desert, and toward the distant mountains.

Lorenzo Oatman, though clubbed and thrown over the ledge, had not been killed. When he regained consciousness and was able to crawl up to the massacre site, the Indians had left, and he found all of his family dead except the two missing girls. Terribly wounded, the boy found some scraps of food, then set out to walk and crawl back along the trail toward the Pima villages. He was sometimes delirious with pain and fear, and when he stopped to rest the coyotes approached so near that he was afraid to sleep but kept waving his hands at them to drive them away.

In the desert near Gila Bend he saw Indians approaching and tried to hide, but they proved to be friendly Maricopas who recognized him as having been in the party camped at Maricopa Wells. They gave him food and water, rode on the flat to find that his story was truthful, then took him back to Maricopa Wells, where he found that the two remaining family groups, the Wilders and the Kelleys, were hitched up and ready to start along the trail to Yuma. Three days later, with Lorenzo lying in one of the wagon beds, they resumed their journey over the desolate road. At the little mesa they stopped to bury the remains of the Oatman family, partially eaten by wild animals, in a common grave. The area was still strewn with the forlorn family possessions the Indians had not taken, the contents of wagons and trunks thrown about and partially burned. Later, the Bartlett expedition, surveying the international boundary between the United States and Mexico, reburied the scattered bones of the unfortunate family. At Fort Yuma, Lorenzo was cared for and remained in the post hospital for two months.

Meanwhile the two captive girls, Olive and Mary Ann, had been driven by their captors into a life of slavery. Usually when captives could not keep up their pace the Indian war parties killed them on the spot, but when Mary Ann could go no further one of the warriors carried her on his back. Her bare feet lacerated and bleeding, Olive managed to stumble along as the Indians raced to escape possible pursuit. The second night one of the cows was killed and roasted over their camp fire. The third night they arrived at their home rancheria, somewhere in the vicinity of Date Creek in the Bradshaw Mountains. There the captive girls were turned over to the squaws to experience a cruelty to which the previous days of travel were nothing.

The girls became drudges for the entire Indian village. They gathered wood, tended the fires, picked grass seeds which was part of the Indian diet, and worked with the squaws at baking mescal. If they were seen to stand idle for a minute, they were beaten. If they were unable to understand what was said to them they were whipped again. Their food was that of the nomadic band, grass seeds, roots, cactus fruits, mescal. When food was scarce they ate worms, grasshoppers, crickets, lizards and rodents. At other times war parties brought in animals from plundered wagon trains, which were eaten and the captives given the scraps. In their misery the girls clung together and even tried to save some food to take should a chance to escape appear, but this plan was abandoned as Mary Ann became weaker.

Periodically bands of Mohave Indians from the Colorado River country came to the Yavapai camp to trade. Soon the girls heard that the Mohaves were trying to buy them, and they hoped they would pass into other hands where they would receive kinder treatment and there was more food. A little more than a year after their capture, they were traded to the Mohaves for two horses, three blankets, some beads and a quantity of vegetables. The girls and their new owners started on a journey that took eleven days, from the Bradshaw Mountains across the desert to the Mohave Valley, and a village on the Colorado River above the Bill Williams fork.

Though still the slaves and drudges of the common tribe, the girls did find life here a little easier. The Mohaves farmed a little along the river, growing maize, corn, melons and wheat, and gathering beans from the mesquite trees which grew in great abundance around the village. The girls were given a small plot of ground on which to grow their own patches of food crops. Like the Yavapais, the Mohaves' supplies of food varied with times of rain and drought. Their chief food was mesquite beans ground into a coarse meal and boiled in water. Every day the slave girls ground mesquite beans, gathered roots, fruits and berries, and received the scantiest portions. They were always hungry.

The first year among the Mohaves was probably their easiest in captivity. The little garden patch they planted reminded them of their farm home. The squaw of the chief took to them in a kindly way and gave them a little more food. One day the medicine man tattooed the captives with a mark similar to that worn by the Mohave women, five vertical blue lines from the mouth down to the chin. It was done by pricking the skin with a very sharp stick until it bled. The stick was then dipped into the juice of a weed, and the powder of a blue stone found in the riverbed. Burned and pulverized, it turned nearly black. The fine powder was pricked into the wounds and left an indelible, blue–black mark. The process was very painful and irreversible. Olive bore these marks the rest of her life.

The second year was another of drought. The slave girls were forced to work harder than ever at food gathering. Many of the Mohaves died, and it became apparent that Mary Ann was becoming weaker and dying, too, of starvation. Olive hunted for food harder than ever, and at night they huddled together and sang the songs they had learned in their family farm to cheer them. One sad day Mary Ann finally died, to the extreme grief of Olive. It was the custom of the Mohaves to cremate their dead, but at the intercession of the wife of the chief Olive was given a blanket in which to wrap her sister's body and allowed to bury it in the little plot of ground that had been their garden.

During the period of their captivity their brother Lorenzo had never given up hope. At Fort Yuma he had made two lasting friends in a Dr. Hewit who attended his wounds, and the post carpenter, Henry Grinnell, the same man who in future years would build and maintain Grinnell's Station on the Butterfield Overland route. He took a keen interest in the fate of the captive girls and promised to continue the search for them. The post commander, Major Heintzelman, could spare no troops to send out as a search party, nor was it certain where the captives had been taken. Lorenzo went on to California where he continued to try to get help. At Fort Yuma, Henry Grinnell kept his ears open and urged others to do the same.

The third year of Olive's captivity among the Mohaves was an abundant one. The Colorado River overflowed, irrigating the fields, and causing a double crop of mesquite beans. Food was plentiful, and in the fall the Indians gave a big feast at the village where Olive was held. Other Indian bands up and down the river were invited to the festivities. During the gambling that attended the feast a Yuma Indian named Antonio Francisco won some horses. He was offered two captive women, Olive and a Cocopah squaw, in place of the horses. Antonio refused and took the horses, but at Fort Yuma he bragged about his winnings and told of the two captive women he had been offered. This was the break Henry Grinnell had been waiting for.

It was decided that gambling would be the safest cover to gain the womens' release. The new post commander, Lt. Col. Martin Burke, and Grinnell gave Antonio two horses, four blankets, some beads and other trinkets to effect Olive's release, and Burke gave Antonio a letter to Olive authorizing her to demand her release in the name of the United States if he should find her. Weeks slipped by with no word from Antonio, and again hope was giving away. But Antonio was doing his work.

At the Mohave Camp he made friends with Olive's captors and gambled with them. At first they thought he had killed some white men and obtained the beads and blankets. He gave the letter to Olive, who had trouble reading it after five years in which she had seen no writing. Then Antonio stated his mission to the Mohaves. They held a long council in which he threatened that, if they did not release Olive, the whole tribe would be wiped out by soldiers from Fort Yuma. At length the Mohaves agreed to let her go. She arrived with Antonio at Fort Yuma on February 22, 1856, and had a moving reunion with Lorenzo who arrived at the fort a short time later.

There have been many stories and rumors about Olive Oatman's life during her captivity and after her release. The truth is that she went to live with relatives in Oregon. A Reverend Royal B. Stratton took an interest in her story and wrote a book, *The Captivity of the Oatman Girls*, that was published in 1857. It proved to be a sensation, and earnings from it financed the education of Olive and Lorenzo and led to the printing of another edition in New York. While lecturing to help with book sales she met Mr. John B. Fairchild, and they were married. In time they moved to Sherman, Texas, where they adopted a child and lived for many years. Olive died at age sixty–five and was buried in Sherman.

She never, as was erroneously printed, was insane, nor did she give birth to a child while in captivity as was later falsely claimed by an Arizona man. She always answered, when asked, that the Indians had never attempted to violate her chastity, nor was she ever the wife of an Indian. The residents of Oatman, Arizona, a mining town near the Colorado River, named their town in honor of her family, and another short–lived town on the Colorado was named Olive City, in honor of Olive herself.

In 1858, seven years after the Oatman tragedy, the Butterfield company began organizing its overland stage line from St. Louis to San Francisco. The southern route ran along the Gila trail, where twenty–six stations were established in Arizona Territory. One of these was at Oatman Flat, run by a man named Jacobs. It is said that the trail itself at this point ran directly over the grave of the Oatman family. Numerous references to the station and the story of the Oatman family are made in journals of travelers over the Gila trail, as Reverend Stratton's book was then at the zenith of its popularity and everyone knew the story. Though Butterfield ceased operations in 1861, travel over the trail continued for many more years, with other references to the spot by later visitors.

After the Civil War regular mail and passenger stagecoaches began rolling over the Gila trail again and the old stations, some of which had been abandoned, came into prominence and prosperity again. The reminiscences of the famous Arizona pioneer William F. (Billy) Fourr tell of his owning what had been Kenyon's Station just east of Oatman Flat on the Butterfield line, then Burk's Station immediately west of Oatman Flat. Mr. Fourr's dates of this period are hazy, but it is generally agreed that it was in 1869 that he sold Burk's and took over the abandoned station at Oatman Flat. He built a stout adobe house, ranched and farmed and raised a family there in addition to running his station. Ruins of the house, and graves of some of the Fourr children enclosed by a little fence and still carefully preserved, are to be seen there today.

...The deserted Oatman Flat station...had been given up as the road was very bad and they had made a better one ten or fifteen miles around," wrote Mr. Fourr. "I spent $5,000 fixing up a more direct road, which would come by the station, made it a toll road, and also charged ten cents a head for water. At that I never got my money back. Sometimes people did not want to pay and would ask me where my charter was. I would tell them that they had come over part of my road and that, if they did not pay, I would show them where my charter was.

I had a charter from the legislature to collect, but the best charter was a double-barreled shotgun.

While in Oatman a little Arab came through with from sixteen to thirty camels, which he had bought from the government cheap. The government, when it gave up its camel experiment, sold some to 'Hi Jolly' and others, and some they turned loose. ('Hi Jolly' was the Western corruption of the name Haj Ali, an Arabian camel driver.) 'Hi Jolly' packed water across the Maricopa Desert, twenty-two gallons on each side of an animal, and sold it to teamsters between Gila Bend and Yuma.

One time he came over my toll road and we all went out to look at them. I charged him fifteen dollars to take the outfit through and he never came back. It was not long after that he stopped using them. Just pulled off the saddles and threw them down and turned the camels loose. They were not a success as the red clay was too hard on their feet.

Billy Fourr records that he sold the Oatman Flat station in 1878 and moved to the Dragoon Mountains, in what would become Cochise County, where he established the famous Fourr F cattle ranch. He knew when to unload the station at the proper time, because by then it was doomed. The railroad was building eastward across Arizona from Yuma, and while it followed approximately the old Gila trail, it did not follow every bend and crook of the Gila River as the trail did. It gradually drew away from the river until at Gila Bend it was eight miles south of it, thus by-passing all of the old stage stations and effectively consigning them to oblivion.

Thus it was at Oatman Flat, which sank back to the peace and solitude of the desert, with the silence broken only by the gurgling of the Gila flowing nearby. The house and road deteriorated as nature began to reclaim her own. If one goes there today, he will find the ruins of the old ranch house and a little plot of farm ground on the sandy flat. Nothing remains of the old station that preceded Billy Fourr's house; it stood in the middle of what is now the field. At the grave of the Oatman family is a little monument erected by people in the little towns nearby who do not want it to be forgotten. While there are people like them, the Oatman family and its travail and that of others like them will not be forgotten, but will live in the hearts of those who cherish the memories of the Old West.

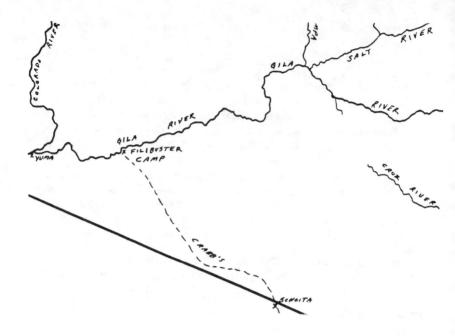

Maps for Chapter 7 - Filibuster Camp

FILIBUSTER CAMP is one of those places that is competely obliterated. Its location was in what are now farms along the Gila River. north of Wellton. Caborca and Altar in Mexico can be reached by way of modern highways in the United States and Mexico. The sketch at right shows Crabb's approximate route, along El Camino Del Diablo to Sonoita, then to Caborca on a course approximately, possibly somewhat east of, Mexican Highway 2.

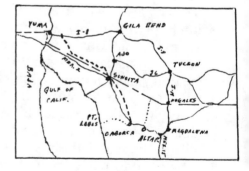

CHAPTER 7
Filibuster Camp

Hearing the word "filibuster" most of us in today's world picture members of Congress holding the floor by talking endlessly, thereby preventing a vote on a bill which they oppose and feel is certain to pass. Yet in the dictionary that is definition number two for the word. The first definition was common in yesterday's world; as a noun it is "an irregular military adventurer, an American fomenting insurrections in Latin America in the mid-nineteenth century" and as a verb "to carry out insurrectionist or revolutionary activities in a foreign country." That was the exact intent of the men who gathered at Filibuster Camp among the mesquite thickets on the old emigrant trail along the Gila River, forty miles east of the Colorado, thirty miles north of the Mexican border.

Their tragic story is found in newspaper accounts of their time, particularly the **Sacramento Union** in May 1857, and others in the files of the Arizona Historical Foundation.

The year was 1857, the setting was the wild remoteness of the Arizona desert, desolate and uninhabited, the perfect place to make plans and train a private army away from the scrutiny of the authorities. To Filibuster Camp early in March came "General" Henry A. Crabb, a title bestowed upon him by his ninety men, after marching overland from San Pedro, California. Well they might camp and train, for they were poorly equipped for the adventure upon which they were about to embark. They were the advance party of a force of a thousand men, who were even then, they believed, being recruited in California to sail to Port Lobos near Caborca, Mexico, from where they would march overland as reinforcements.

Henry Crabb was then in his thirties, handsome and personable, a man well-known in California where he had even aspired to a seat in the United States Senate. He was married to a member of the Ainsa family, prominent in the affairs of the state of Sonora in northern Mexico, bordering the United States. Much of Mexico was then in a near-feudal state, still unsettled after wars resulting in defeat and loss of territory to Texas, to the United States in 1848, and further loss due to the Gadsden Purchase of 1853. Most of the people were poor; thousands of the men had emigrated to the California gold fields after the discoveries there in 1849, so that in many Mexican villages there were few men.

Sonora was also a seething hot-bed of racial and nationalistic hatreds, fanned by constant atrocities committed by all of the various groups against the others. First was the Apache Indians, whose murderous forays gained them the hatred of Mexicans and Americans alike. Failing to pacify the Apaches over centuries, the Mexicans had initiated campaigns of extermination against them, which also failed. Mexicans and Apaches, and later Americans, sometimes slaughtered each other on sight without compunction. In the aftermath of warfare Americans, especially Texans, held Mexicans in contempt which was returned by them in full measure. Mexican bandits and adventurers murdered Americans at will, and the shooting of a Mexican by an American was a thing of so little notice that he did not even file a notch in his gun handle record of killings. Often the bodies of those killed were simply left unburied, by all factions, to be fed upon by wild animals or just rot away.

The Crabb expedition was not the first to attempt to take advantage of the chaotic conditions in northern Mexico. Several others had tried but not succeeded in attempts to establish their own private countries or states. Bands of American outlaws roved the area, killing and looting at will. One of these had occurred only a few years prior to Crabb's expedition, and hatreds generated by it led in part to the fate that befell Crabb. One Parker H. French with twenty-five Americans had traveled through Sonora. At the little town of Cieneguita in western Sonora they were welcomed by the priest of the little church. They answered by hanging him by the neck to force him to tell where his treasure was hidden. To save the priest's life, his sisted disclosed the location. The Americans sacked the town and ravished every woman regardless of age before continuing on their way unpunished.

It was against this background of hostilities and political unrest that Crabb with his wife visited some socially prominent families in Sonora in 1856. Senor Manuel Gandara was then the political overlord of Sonora, but a ruthless revolutionary named Ignacio Pesqueira was plotting to overthrow Gandara and take over the government himself. Crabb met Pesqueira and fell into a political intrigue with him. He agreed to raise an army of a thousand men in the United States to fight with Pesqueira. After the overthrow of Gandara, Crabb was to receive lands and mineral rights in Mexico bordering the United States, in return for protection from Apache raids.

Crabb returned to California to get on with his part of the bargain. There were plenty of adventurers and freebooters on the California frontier ready and anxious to join his expedition, of which the American and state governments had full knowledge. The advance party of ninety men was quickly recruited and set out for Mexico by way of Filibuster Camp. A 'General' John D. Cosby was left in San Francisco to raise the remainder of the thousand-man army, but unknown to Crabb he made no effort to do so. There were rumors of evidence that he instead enriched himself with funds entrusted to him for that purpose. Upon reaching Filibuster Camp, Crabb sent 'Major' Robert Wood and 'Major' Charles Tozer to Tucson to raise additional recruits there with results that shall be seen.

Late in March, then, eighty-nine men left Filibuster Camp for Sonoita just across the Mexican border and their eventual destination of the city of Altar deeper in Sonora. Most of their transportation was by pack mules; there was one wagon carrying ammunition. The rough volcanic country and lack of water in the inhospitable desert told heavily on the little force, and at Cabeza Prieta halfway to Sonoita twenty men were separated to proceed more slowly while the rest went on ahead. Much of the supplies they had cached was stolen by Mexican emigrants, and many of their animals died from exhaustion and lack of water. Soon they struck the infamous Camino Del Diablo, the 'Devil's Highway,' littered with the bones of men and animals that perished along this blazing desert trail, but all of the men eventually arrived at Sonoita.

Crabb there made a confounding discovery and a fatal error. The rebel, Pesqueira, had already overthrown Gandara and was now the governor of Sonora. He no longer needed Crabb's aid, and indeed to acknowledge that Crabb was allied with him in any way would have quickly undermined his newly-won position, causing his immediate overthrow and possible execution. Pesqueira at once denounced the Crabb expedition as American interlopers and warned that it not advance further into Mexico.

Crabb and his men, however, were not easily discouraged. They were confident that, with reinforcements expected from

San Francisco for certain and possibly from Tucson, they could take and hold the land they had expected and still coveted. Crabb decided to advance to Caborca, 110 miles to the south. He sent a threatening letter to the prefect of the Altar district announcing his attention to advance and occupy the territory peacefully if possible, but threatening to fight for it if need be. This letter was dated March 26, 1857. Pesqueira immediately replied with a call to arms to the Sonoran people. It began with "Ignacio Pesqueira, Substitute Governor of the State and Commander of the Chief of the Frontier, to his fellow citizens: Free Sonoranians! To arms all!!" and ended with "Viva Mexico! Death to the Filibusters!"

On March 30th Crabb with his force now numbering sixty-nine men left Sonoita for Caborca. He left instructions that the twenty men who were following because of injury or illness were to proceed to Caborca with all speed their condition would permit to join him. Sixteen of the twenty followed these orders, four who were too ill to travel remaining in Sonoita. Crabb's advance force came to Caborca on April first, where about a quarter-of-a-mile from the town a few soldiers were drawn up in formation before them. Suddenly the Mexicans fired on the Americans, who were not expecting such a welcome. The firing caused some consternation and confusion among Crabb's men, but did practically no damage. The Americans then returned the fire, killing ten or fifteen of the Mexicans. One of them was the commander, Lorenzo Rodriguez, who according to some accounts was coming out to speak with Crabb.

At this the Mexicans retreated to the town's most redoubtable building, an ancient but splendid mission church, much like the San Xavier mission in Arizona. The remaining buildings in Caborca were merely adobe houses, many of them hovels or huts. Military experts say that Crabb should have charged and taken the church immediately, and would have won the battle then and there. The populace except for the men in the church with few exceptions had fled the town for the nearby hills. Crabb's force instead occupied several of the adobe houses across the narrow street across from the church.

On the second day of the stalemate it is said that the Mexicans offered to allow Crabb's force to depart for the border, and some within the expedition felt that they could still fight their way free and return to the United States. Most were still certain that they could win the fight and continue on their course. The

Mexicans who had fled, however, gradually returned to the town, emboldened by the apparent entrapment of the Americans. Gradually they circled Crabb's position, and now he was trapped.

Crabb then called for volunteers for an assault on the church, fifteen men including Crabb himself responding. They charged across the street under heavy fire and forced the Mexicans occupying the covent connected to the church to flee into the main church building. A keg of powder was set against the door into the mission with the intent to blow it open, but the match used to light the fuse was damp. Before another suitable match could be found, the Mexicans counter-attacked the convent. After severe hand-to-hand fighting in which two Americans were killed and others including Crabb wounded, the Americans were forced to retreat from the convent to the houses across the street.

For four days the fighting continued, with the plight of Crabb's force being more and more desperate, and the ring of steel gradually tightening around them. One of the Americans, on the pretext of going into the yard for water, sprang over the fence and ran down the street in an attempt to desert to the Mexicans. He was captured, tortured to make him disclose conditions in the houses, and then executed. By breaking through the walls of houses the Mexicans finally forced the Americans into one house on the corner of the plaza. Then on April sixth Mexican reinforcements arrived from Altar with two small cannon.

With these the Mexicans tried to batter down the door to the house which Crabb held, but their charges were not strong enough to even beat the door down. Finally, Papago Indians arched flaming arrows down upon the thatched roof of Crabb's fortress, setting the roof on fire. Unable to fight the fire without exposing themselves to Mexican bullets, Crabb's men set off kegs of powder hoping to blow the fire out. In this they partially succeeded, but suffered severe effects themselves from the blasts. Their situation now desperate, the Americans had to decide whether to try to fight their way out or surrender.

Crabb's men were deeply divided on that decision. Some were sure that surrender meant certain death, and they wanted to fight on while attempting to escape. Others were sure that they would be treated as prisoners of war if they surrendered and their lives spared. Under a white flag one of the men was sent to ask terms of the Mexicans. He was not allowed to return, but forced to shout across the street the terms of his captors. The Americans were told that if they surrendered they would be taken to Altar and tried as prisoners of war, and that the wounded among them would be treated. Crabb at length agreed to those terms of surrender.

It was eleven o'clock at night when Crabb was the first to surrender. He was taken aside. One by one the remaining 58 Americans came out, their hands were bound in front of them, they were searched, and held in a barracks building. There were no incidents during the surrender, and all the Americans expected to be released within a short time. During the night a Mexican came to where the Americans were being held and delivered a paper. To their consternation and dread it was their sentence, which was to be executed at sunrise. Only one was to be spared, a sixteen year old boy, whose life was claimed by the deputy commander of the garrison. He was eventually released.

At sunrise the Americans were taken in groups of five to ten to the outskirts of the cemetery and massacred. It is said that they went to their deaths so calmly and bravely that their murderers could not bear to face them, and they were forced to turn around and be shot in the back. Their bodies were stripped naked and were not buried, simply allowed to lie on the ground to rot. Hogs of the villagers fed upon the carcasses. After some days a shallow trench was dug, and whatever remained was shoved into it and covered with earth.

Crabb himself was allowed to write letters to his wife and other members of his family, and at length taken to the plaza where his arms were extended above his head and tied to a pillar. A hundred bullets fired into his back took his life. As his body hung suspended, Crabb's head was cut off and preserved in a jar of tequila, then put on display as an object of public scorn.

The sixteen men who had followed Crabb from Sonoita arrived later on the day of the massacre. One of their number advanced into town to inquire concerning Crabb's whereabouts, no one suspecting anything of what had befallen him. These sixteen met the same fate as those who had gone before them. Hearing that there were others still in Sonoita, the Mexican authorities sent some men to capture them for questioning. The four Americans remaining in Sonoita because they were too ill to follow recrossed the line to the United States side, where they were domiciled in the home of one H. H. Dunbar, who also had a store nearby. On April 17th the Mexicans sought them out, massacred them in the same fashion as the others, and left their bodies unburied on American soil. Friendly Papago Indians buried them, and Dunbar himself escaped death only by being away on business at the time.

Meanwhile, what of 'Majors' Robert Wood and Charles Tozer who had been sent from Filibuster Camp to Tucson to raise additional forces? In Tucson and Calabasas, now a ghost town near Nogales, they conscripted twenty-six men, two of whom are worthy of more than passing mention. One of them was Granville H. Oury, Southern sympathizer, Indian fighter, businessman and politician. Another was John G. Capron, prominent businessman and at one time part owner of the stagecoach line that traversed southern Arizona. Apparently they looked upon this as mostly a business venture, and upon Crabb as entering Sonora at the invitation of several prominent Mexican families.

So thinking, the party left Arizona on April first, bound for Caborca to join Crabb. They were utterly astonished when within sight of the town they were confronted with a force of four hundred Mexicans and Indians. The commander gave them ten minutes in which to surrender or be killed. The Americans instead dismounted, left their pack animals and horses, and descended a bluff in the Altar River bottom to find shelter in a thicket of mesquite trees. When the Mexicans fired on them, the Americans returned fire so effectively that some of the Mexican force was killed, and the rest turned and fled.

In the confusion Oury and three others were separated from the remainder of the group. Some made their way to within a quarter-of-a-mile of the town, where they ascertained that Crabb was not only not in charge of the town, but was under siege. They then began the journey back to American soil nearly a hundred miles away, through hostile territory, and on foot. The return journey was one of incredible hardships, of hunger and thirst, fighting their way. Four of their number were killed in the final dash to the border. There they found that Oury and his three companions were safe, having already reached the border before them.

Thus ended tragically and ingloriously the last of the major filibustering expeditions by Americans into Mexico.

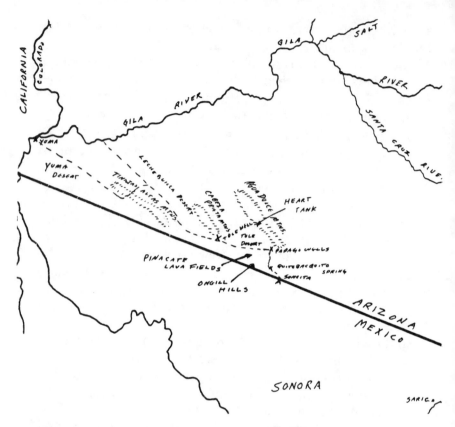

Maps for Chapter 8 - The Devil's Highway

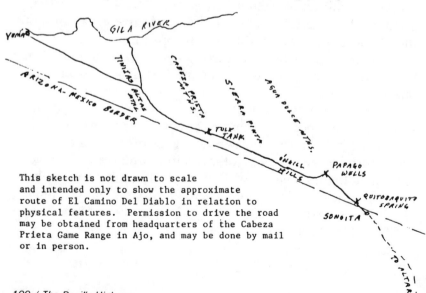

This sketch is not drawn to scale
and intended only to show the approximate
route of El Camino Del Diablo in relation to
physical features. Permission to drive the road
may be obtained from headquarters of the Cabeza
Prieta Game Range in Ajo, and may be done by mail
or in person.

CHAPTER 8
The Devil's Highway

We travelers of today, accustomed to our comfortable high-speed airplanes, trains and autos that whisk us in absolute comfort from one place to another in minutes or hours seldom, if ever, pause to reflect on travel without them. From the very beginning of the coming of man to the earth until only one hundred years ago travel was only carried on by three very different ways unthinkable to us—on foot, riding on a beast such as a horse, mule or donkey, or in a vehicle drawn by such a beast. Until only one hundred and a few years ago!

Even less do we think about our railways and highways, stretching everywhere, smooth as the surface of a pond on a still day, canyons and streams conveniently bridged for us. It is hard for us to even imagine a bumpy and rutted unpaved road, struggling down the side of one canyon and up the other, fording a river with an animal swimming beneath you, or swimming it yourself, or trying to float a wagon across while trying to keep it, with all your worldly possessions, from sinking. Worst of all were desert crossings, the road indefinite because of shifting sand dunes, wandering from one waterhole to another, where often the traveler found that the water had dried up or soaked away. When that happened the traveler and his animals faced almost certain death. In Arizona Territory there was such a road. It fully earned the name given it by the Mexicans, El Camino del Diablo, 'the Devil's highway.'

The road began at the Mexican village of Sonoita, on the Arizona border, and ran west by northwesterly approximately one hundred twenty-five miles to where the City of Yuma now is located. For a long distance it ran only one-half-mile to a few miles north of the present international boundary, closely following it on the American side. It detoured to wells and waterholes, but passed south of the low, barren, harshly rugged desert mountain ranges, staying as much as possible to the level desert. It passed the Agua Dulce Mountains, the Sierra Pinta, and Cabeza Prieta, turned northwest to pass east of the Tinajas Altas and Gila Mountains to strike the Gila River near present-day Wellton and follow it westward to the Colorado River. A variation of the road threaded a pass in the Tinajas Altas and struck northwesterly across the Yuma Desert. From Sonoita the road crossed the rough Pinacate lava flow that destroyed feet, hooves and wheels, the Tule Desert, the Lechuguilla Desert, and the Yuma Desert if one chose that route, all regions of the vast Sonoran Desert of northern Mexico and southern Arizona and California.

It wasn't that men chose that route over others; there were no others, if your destination was the land called California. Travelers might go east of Sonoita a hundred and twenty-five miles to the sometimes flowing Santa Cruz River, follow it north to the Gila, then westerly along that river to the Colorado, hundreds of miles out of the way. They might go west to the shore of the Gulf of California with its salt water and struggle northward over an even worse desert route with no drinking water. It is no wonder at all that travelers from northern Mexico chose to chance the desert road from Sonoita to the Gila River. At twenty miles a day it was a five-day journey, and if it was any season but summer and travelers found the waterholes, if there was water, if nothing broke down, if no person or animal became sick, then the traveler was home free and clear—and extremely lucky. If it was very hot, or there was any emergency, death became probable rather than possible.

No doubt the first to travel the route were the hardy desert Indians, traders from tribes familiar to us such as the Pimas, Papagos and Yumas, some unfamiliar as the Quiquimas, the Cutganes and the Cocopahs. All of them lived in the desert or regions bordering it. Of necessity they knew every waterhole and spring. They lurked near them and killed for food the desert deer and bighorn sheep that watered there. When the Spanish conquerors and colonizers wanted to cross the desert to seek an overland route to California, the Indians were their guides.

The first white man to cross the forbidding desert on this route was the Spanish explorer, Melchior Diaz, in 1540. It would be one hundred sixty years before there would be another. Little was known of the vast Sonoran Desert and the regions west of it. Explorers by sea had touched the west coast of North America, at a land called California. While there were settlements in Baja California, no exploration to the north had been made, and it was almost universally believed that California was an island.

The travels of an exploring priest, Father Eusebio Kino, and

Grave marker on El Camino del Diablo, "The Devil's Highway," north of Tinajas Altas, 1958. (Copyright Wayne Winters, Courtesy Arizona Historical Society)

his escort, Captain Juan Manje, in 1699 led Kino to conclude that the Baja was a peninsula, that the land of California was not an island, and a land route to it was possible. From Sonora to the California side of the Colorado River Kino traveled three times, over the route of 'the Devil's highway,' guided by the Indians. His journal was to become the guidebook of explorers who were to follow.

Spanish colonies were established at San Diego and Monterey in 1769. They had to be kept supplied by sea, however, so a land route was badly needed. Another exploring priest, Father Francisco Garces, had reached the Colorado River by way of the Santa Cruz River to the Gila River, thence along the Gila to the Colorado. He was convinced that Kino had been correct in asserting that there was a land route to California. When in 1774 Captain Juan De Anza assembled an exploring party of twenty volunteer soldiers and a few others to find a California overland trail, Garces was in it.

De Anza had planned to follow the trail along the Santa Cruz and Gila Rivers but the Apache Indians raided his corrals and stole his horses. Rather than risk further brushes with the Apaches, De Anza led his party to Sonoita, thence across the desert route from Sonoita to the Gila River, following the trail of Kino seventy-five years earlier. De Anza's mission was successful, the land route to the California colonies was established, but his ensuing trips with colonists, their flocks and possessions were over the Santa Cruz-Gila Rivers route.

The desert trail followed by Kino and De Anza varied somewhat from the later route of El Camino del Diablo when it earned that name. Evidently they started due west from Sonoita, along the Sonoita River, for some distance before heading northward. Along the river for some distance there were small settlements, and of course running water. Their first desert watering place may have been Papago Wells, at the north end of the Agua Dulce Mountains. De Anza mentions going west through a "white pass" in the hills, which was through the O'Neill Hills between Papago Wells and the Tule Desert. The hills were named in later years for prospector Dave O'Neill. When his burros arrived at Papago Wells without him, a search party went out, trailing the burros. They found poor Dave, dead of dehydration and exposure, and buried him in the hills that bear his name.

Beyond the hills on the Tule Desert, Kino and De Anza stayed along the western fringe of the Sierra Pinta Mountains, rather than heading immediately west. Their reason was water, a large natural tank in the rocks high up in a canyon, that filled when it rained and seldom dried up between rains. There was a hard climb to reach it, for animals or men, sometimes reached only by climbing on hands and knees. Kino named it Aguaje de la Luna (Moonlight Water), De Anza called it Agua Empinado. Now it is known as Tinaja del Corazon (Heart Tank) because at certain water levels the tank's surface is heart-shaped.

From here Kino and De Anza's routes varied. De Anza's next water was across the Tule Desert on the east side of the Cabeza Prieta (Black Head) range, where he found six natural tanks, filled with rainwater, ascending the rocky slopes. Water from the higher tanks drained into the lower, and it was possible to water a thousand animals in a short time, since they were so large. De Anza called them the Tinajas (Tanks) de la Purificacion.

They are now called the Cabeza Prieta Tanks, a rare natural phenomenon. The large, kettle-shaped tanks, worn out of the solid rock over thousands of years, descend one to another connected by a natural waterway that drains one tank into another. It is estimated they hold 5,000 gallons of water, and are seldom emptied by evaporation before rains refill them.

Kino and De Anza's route, as was that of the El Camino del Diablo, circled the south end of the Cabeza Prieta Mountains and across the Lechuguilla (Agave) Desert to the Tinajas Altas (High Tanks) Mountains. Here again water was to be found in natural rock tanks. Kino stopped at a tank he called Agua Escondida, but finding little water pressed on early the next day to the "good tank" of the Tinajas Altas. Here again he found plenty of water in the natural rock tanks. from there it was a journey of fifteen leagues (a league being two-and-a-half miles) north to the Gila River and the westward trail to the Colorado.

De Anza camped in a canyon, having crossed the Lechuguilla Desert, where he had some wells dug in the sand. They filled with enough water to care for his needs. He called them Pozos de en Media (Half-way Wells), and the next day did not even stop at the Tinajas Altas tanks. He threaded his way through a pass in the Tinajas Altas and headed straight across the desert for the confluence of the Gila and Colorado Rivers at what is now Yuma. En route they camped at Pozo Blando (Sweetwater Well) which was known to Father Garces, before reaching the Colorado River.

After De Anza's time another seventy-five years went by before two events turned the sporadic travel over the desert trail into a torrent of humanity and earned it for all time its notorious name of 'the Devil's highway.' The first event was the treaty in 1848 ending the war between the United States and Mexico, giving the United States all of California and of Arizona Territory north of the Gila River. The second event was the discovery that same year of gold at Sutter's Mill in California, precipitating the gold rush of 1849.

Again it is difficult for us in this time to imagine the impact that the discovery of gold in California had on that time. Our usual perception is that gold seekers from eastern cities rushed westward along the trails, braving the terrain, the Indians and the elements, and that many of them died along the way, all too true. We do not realize the electric effect the discovery had on other nations as well. Gold seekers rushed from all over the world, from Europe, from the Orient, from South America—and more importantly to our narrative from the new state of Texas and from Old Mexico. Many cities in Texas and Mexico were nearly depopulated of young men, caught up in the whirlwind toward the California gold fields. The shortest route was across northern Mexico and 'the Devil's highway.'

There were other routes, of course. Fairly safe were those on ships to the Isthmus of Panama, a trip on horseback across the Isthmus, and sailing from there to the California seaports, principally San Francisco. From southern Texas and Mexican cities travelers could make their way to the ports on Mexico's west coast and try to book passage on a ship sailing from there. For impatient gold rushers that was not good enough. Individually, or in parties of two or three to a dozen, or in long wagon trains with extra horses and mules they set out over the land routes to travel at their own forced paces, eager to be the first to the gold fields.

From interior cities such as San Luis Potosi, Durango, Monterrey and Parras the Mexicans could go north to Parral, and northwesterly over the old mission routes past Santa Ana or through Chihuahua toward the Arizona border. From southern Texas cities gold rushers could cross the Rio Grande at Laredo, Eagle Pass, and other border towns to follow the Mexican routes through Parras or Chihuahua. From the north they could cross at El Paso and take the Mexican roads westward through Corralitos and Janos, thus avoiding the territory of the fierce Apache Indians, who would contest their advance every step of the way. Nearing the U.S. border a choice had to be made—follow the trails along the Santa Cruz and Gila Rivers and again risk battling the Apaches, or take the old mission roads to Sonoita, thence to California over Kino and De Anza's desert trail. Unaware of its danger, thousands chose the desert trail. Those who lived would learn to curse it as 'the Devil's highway.'

Over the years the trail became a desert road, still discernable and it can be traveled today. From Sonoita it led to Quitobaquito spring, where there is a waterhole, half-a-mile north of the international border. There are a number of explanations for that name, the most likely being that it was named after the Mexican village of Quitobac located some distance below the border. "Quito" meaning "little" and "bac" a Papago word for "spring," it is likely that the adding of a final "quito" to the name of the town gave us "little Quitobac." Ringed by cottonwoods, the spring and waterhole are there today in the Organ Pipe Cactus National Monument.

The next water was at Papago Wells, northwest of Quitobaquito, then the trail passed through O'Neill's Hills and crossed the Tule (Reed) Desert to Tule Well at the south end of the Cabeza Prieta range. At the end of the Cabeza Prietas it ran as always, across the Lechuguilla Desert to the tanks of the Tinajas Altas, and so on across the Lechuguilla Desert to the Gila River or the Yuma Desert to the Colorado.

Of course the gold rushers were warned of the danger. Kino and De Anza had traveled it in the winter months when the weather was mildest and the infrequent rains still most frequent, with Indians who knew the way to guide them. Not so the gold rushers. They recklessly plunged ahead regardless of the time of year, the heat, or the probable availability of water. If someone else had made it, so could they. They had no one to guide them to the hidden rock tanks. They knew nothing of the devastatingly dehydrating effects of the desert sun, and temperatures rising to one hundred and twenty degrees. They discounted stories of the rugged barrens of the Pinacate lava beds or the shifting sand dunes of the desert.

Hundreds of them died along 'the Devil's highway.' They missed the waterholes and tanks. Their vehicles broke down. Men and animals became sick, and there was no place to rest and recover. Even those who followed or went on rescue missions put themselves at risk to try to aid the stricken. When water supplies ran out they simply laid down and died, men and animals alike. The wreckage of wagons and the whitened bones littered the roadside almost the length of the trail. Graves covered with stones and with rude markers were to be seen all along the road. It was said that as many as fifty travelers arrived at the Tinajas Altas tanks, found the bottom tanks dry, and were too weak to climb to water at the upper tanks. They perished, and were buried on a bluff east of the mountains.

From the traffic on it at the gold rush's height travel on the desert road gradually dwindled. The world's great rush of civilization passed it by, leaving it in grim and unyielding solitude. Still over the last one hundred years and even today there are those who travel it. Some are men who administer the game range established there to preserve the habitat of the desert animals, principally the bighorn sheep, digging out and improving the natural waterholes and tanks. Some are wary and travel at night, hiding by day, known as illegal aliens. Some are adventurers, longing to travel the old trails, stepping in the footprints of the famed conquistadores and exploring priests. A few have sought treasure.

There are two tales of El Camino del Diablo that have a connection with that magic word, "treasure." The first was a theory developed by Mr. Paul V. Lease of California, published with permission of his widow after Mr. Lease's death in 1963. His theory was that the Pima Indian revolt against Spanish rule in 1751, when all of the missions in Pimeria Alta were burned and all the colonists, soldiers and priests slain, was actually plotted and abetted by wealthy Spanish landowners. They had reason to believe that the Jesuit priests at the missions had hidden gold mines, the treasure from which was stored at secret vaults at the missions. From there, supposedly, it was transported by burro trains to ports on the Gulf of California and secretly loaded on ships bound for Spain. Smuggled into Spain to escape confiscation or taxation by the king, it vastly enriched the treasury of the Jesuit order.

One of the missions said to have a secret vault was that at Sonoita, at the eastern end of El Camino del Diablo. The night before the uprising on November 21, 1751, an unsuspecting priest loaded a burro train from the treasure vault there under cover of darkness. Before dawn he started with it toward the gulf, westward along the trail that became 'the Devil's highway.' Camped at the Quitobaquito spring that night, the priest saw a large, orange ball on the horizon of the evening sky in the direction of Sonoita. There was no mistaking the meaning of such a huge light. Sonoita was burning and only an Indian uprising could have caused it. In the morning he knew that vengeful Pimas would set out in pursuit of him and his treasure.

Quick and drastic action would be needed to save his life, his companions and the gold. The priest headed the burro train northwest to Papago Wells, the next water. From there, rather than heading west on the trail to eventually veer southward to the gulf, the treasure train went northward along the eastern slopes of the Sierra Pinta range. To the north were secret treasure trails and waterholes, and mountain canyons in which to hide until the uprising was crushed. It was his only hope.

Under orders from their chief, a party of the Pimas in revolt had set out after the burro train. On the trail to Quitobaquito it met some Papago Indians, late arriving for the revolt. From them the Pimas learned that the burros were only a few hours ahead, and the Papagos joined the pursuing Pimas. At Papago Wells the pursuers learned that the burro train had left an hour earlier. Pausing only long enough to refresh themselves, the Pimas set out again, expecting to catch up in two hours. Suddenly they held up. Trail signs told them that a large, far-westward ranging band of Apache Indian raiders had found the tracks of the burro train and was now following it. The small Pima band felt itself no match for the larger Apache party, so it hid in an arroyo to await developments.

Up ahead the priest had ordered the burros into the mountains. He halted the train and ordered the gold unloaded, carried up a slope, and stacked beside and behind a large boulder. This task was not quite finished when the Apaches attacked. The waiting Pimas heard gunfire, and saw a cloud of dust from the hooves of a large herd of animals being driven north. When all was quiet, the Pimas took up the trail again. At its end was only deadly silence. The dead and mutilated bodies of all those with the burro train lay all around. There were a few dead animals. The gold lay where it had been stacked, or had fallen when the Apaches attacked.

Having no way to transport the gold, the Pimas left it, and reported its location to their chief. When the revolt was put down, the chief used his knowledge of the location of the gold as a bargaining tool to escape punishment. Mr. Lease's theory concludes, however, that the Pimas never revealed the location of the treasure, and it is still there in a canyon of the Sierra Pintas to be found and claimed. Even if one granted the detailed accuracy of Mr. Lease's theory, it would be hard to agree that the treasure had escaped notice for almost two hundred fifty years of the Spanish, the Pimas and Papagos, sharp-eyed prospectors and treasure hunters.

The second tale of treasure along El Camino del Diablo was recorded by Arizona pioneer and historian Roscoe G. Willson in a book published in 1958. It concerns a ledge of gold said to have been found, then lost by a Mexican known only as El Jabonero (The Soapmaker). No other name for him has ever been found. Directions to the ledge were given, according to Willson, to a man named John Cameron by a treasure seeker who had failed to find it. "This queerly worded document, tattered and torn, yellowed with age, and barely decipherable," wrote Mr. Willson, "was given me by John Cameron at Ajo, on January 29, 1948, and the next day I stood on the little hill at Quitobaquito and gazed across the desert to the shimmering hills and mountains, any one of which might hold the secret of El Jabonero. It is a lonely, desolate land."

The tale of El Jabonero began in 1849, when a party of Sonorans including him started for the California gold fields from the small settlement of La Cienega, just a little south of the Arizona border. The party camped for the night a short distance from Quitobaquito, turning their horses loose to graze. The next day El Jabonero's horse was missing, and he set out to follow its tracks. Evidently the horse was a traveler, because he followed it several miles to the northwest before spotting it from the top of a small hill. Starting after it, he removed a rock from his huaraches (shoes) and found his foot was on a ledge of rock sparkling with gold.

Knocking off some of the rock, El Jabonero hastened to Quitobaquito, where it was pounded out and a cupful of gold obtained. Giving up thoughts of California, El Jabonero returned to La Cienega where he obtained a prospecting outfit and two companions to help him. On their way to the ledge their camp was attacked one morning by "Arenena Indians." El Jabonero and one other man were killed. The other man escaped into the darkness and managed to flee back to La Cienega. He was too frightened to go back to attempt to find the gold.

A few years later this man turned up in California, now under the name of El Jabonero himself. He had been married and had a daughter. He told the story of the lost ledge to his employer. The new El Jabonero could not be persuaded to go back to the desert and guide a search for it, however, and really did not know the location of the ledge though he pretended he did. At last the new El Jabonero made an agreement with his employer. He drew up a document containing "directions" and an appeal to the finder of the ledge to "help my daughter." With this in hand the employer made several unsuccessful attempts to locate the ledge. He then gave the document to John Cameron.

The document, dated 1878 and printed in Mr. Willson's book, betrays the fact that the new El Jabonero knew nothing of the ledge's location. His directions led from Quitobaquito spring around the ends of the Sierra Pinta and Cabeza Prieta ranges,following exactly the route of 'the Devil's highway.' Past the Cabeza Prieta heading for the Tinajas Altas, the directions tell one to stand at the fork in the road, one trail from which leads through the Tinajas Altas, the other heading up the valley to the Gila River. From this fork, to the right, are said to be "three peaks standing along. . .and in directions to said peaks, the middle one is the mine on the opposite side of it." No doubt there is such a fork in the road, as it does divide at Tinajas Altas. However, it is seventy-five miles from Quitobaquito spring, too far for a Mexican to walk in one morning in search of his horse.

After all these years of dwindling use the old trail can still be discerned, and is occasionally traveled, as we have noted. Mexican Highway 2 circumvents it to the south, U.S. Interstate 8 to the north. To a modern traveler in a four-wheel drive vehicle on a winter day the old, faintly-winding desert road might be a pleasant day's drive. But in midsummer, with the temperatures soaring to a hundred and twenty degrees, the waterholes drying up, and the ravens and buzzards circling overhead, it will always be for the unwary 'the Devil's highway.'

Cabeza Prieta tanks in the Cabeza Prieta Mountains near El Camino del Diablo, "The Devil's Highway." Man is unidentified.
(Courtesy Arizona Historical Society))

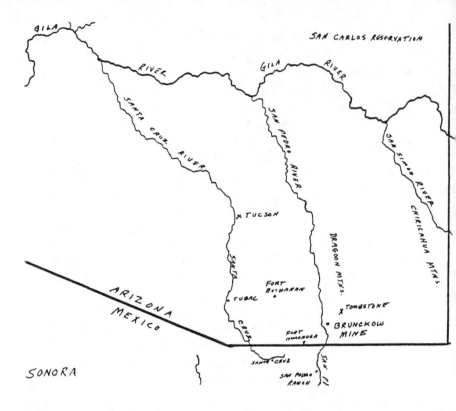

Maps for Chapter 9 - Brunckow Mine

Please do not disturb
this historic spot in
any way.

West of Tombstone on the
Charleston Road, approx.
3/4 mi. from the San Pedro
River, the old Brunckow
Cabin shell can be seen
across an arroyo to the
south.

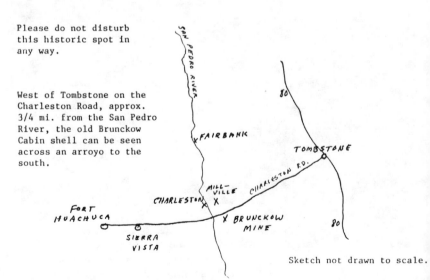

Sketch not drawn to scale.

CHAPTER 9
Brunckow Mine

Should you ever visit old Tombstone, the town of Arizona Territory fame, and by some chance leave it driving westerly to Fort Huachuca, you'll take the Charleston Road. It doesn't seem to have any other road designation, and is called that because in Tombstone's palmy days it connected that city and the satellite town of Charleston on the San Pedro River, nine miles away. As you drive, the scenery, like as not, will not inspire you. The hills of silver through which you drive are unimpressive, brown and greasewood-covered. In the bowels of those hills are the great silver mines that brought Tombstone to its heights when it had more people than all the other towns in the territory combined, and brought it crashing down when the mines flooded with water faster than it could be pumped out. All along both sides of the road are little fallen-in shafts and faded workings of once-promising mining claims that broke the wallets and hearts of their owners.

In a few minutes you will come to the heights overlooking the San Pedro River. In the valley is a ribbon of green, fed by the meandering San Pedro. On its opposite bank, mercifully shrouded by the palo verdes and mesquites, are the remains of the bare adobe walls of the ghost town of Charleston. In it once was the huge Corbin Mill that recovered the silver treasure of the Grand Central Mine in the hills to the north. Off to your right are the remains of the once-great mill of the Tombstone Mining and Milling Company that reduced the ore from the mines owned by the prospector that discovered the Tombstone mines, Ed Schieffelin, and his partners.

Now you must slow down and look quickly to the south, on the other side of the road, or you'll miss it. Some two hundred yards off the road, about three-fourths of a mile from the river, are the ruined buildings and tailings dumps of one of Arizona's most famous mines, the Brunckow Mine. Steeped in tragedy and stained with the blood of prominent men who died for it, rich in history and tradition and legend, one would be certain that the Brunckow Mine was a store of treasure that enriched all who came into possession of it. Yet no less an authority than Jeanne DeVere, Research Historian for the Tombstone Restoration Commission, in a paper written for the Arizona Historical Society in 1960 wrote, "Though many men have given their lives for the Brunckow Mine which has been located and re-located throughout the years the mine has proven absolutely worthless."

The mine which took its name from its association with a famous man named Frederick Brunckow was first known as the 'San Pedro Mine.' It has also been known by other names, corruptions of the name 'Brunckow,' such as Brunkow, Bronkow, Bronco, Broncho and others. Further, writings about the mine range from hazy to downright silent on what kind of mine it was. It would be supposed that, in a region of some of the richest silver mines ever discovered, the Brunckow was also a silver mine. But Richard J. Hinton's *Handbook to Arizona* first published in 1878 that lists all Arizona mines and charts other information about them says not word about the mine or its minerals other than listing its name.

Hinton's "Handbook" carries one paragraph of some illumination, however: "Although there are some indications that mining operations were carried on here by the Jesuits and others, in the seventeenth century, it is not until 1748 that the records become definite. In that year the San Pedro gold mine, it is known, was worked by the Spaniards. . ." It would be the eastern-most of the Jesuit mines in that case, and could not have been heavily worked because of the depredations of the Apache Indians. The Apaches forced abandonment of mines far more westerly and southerly than the San Pedro mine, and well into the nineteenth century.

In the files of the Arizona Historical Foundation in the Hayden Library at Arizona State University in Tempe is a letter from a correspondent of a California newspaper which sheds some light, yet leaves some mystery, on the discovery of the mine: "In company with the distinguished chemist and mineralogist, F. Brunckow, Esq., I visited last week the San Pedro Mine to which I have before alluded in my letters. It is situated within three-fourths of a mile from the river at a point about twenty miles north of the boundary line between Arizona and Sonora (Mexico). . . We spent one day at the mine enjoying the hospitalities of Mr. J. H. Thompson, the original discoverer, and an examination of the evidence which he points out leaves little doubt that the mine was known in former times; but as yet no indications have been found that shows that it was ever before worked." It need not be pointed out that the above and the paragraph from Hinton's "Handbook" seem to be contradictory.

The correspondent's letter continues, "The mine was discovered accidentally by Mr. Thompson sometime last summer. He was riding up the ravine when he dropped his spur, and dismounting, he sat down upon a rock to replace it. As it was during the rainy season, a recent freshet had washed away the earth and left the rock upon which he was sitting quite exposed, and he observed peculiarities about it which induced him to examine further. . . The shaft of the mine has been opened to the depth of fifteen feet, and the ore is much richer than at the surface." [No mention of what kind of ore.] "The vein thus far varies from two feet to one yard in width and will average thirty inches. It promises to be the most valuable mine yet discovered in Arizona, but a sufficient depth has not yet been attained to pronounce upon it with certainty."

The above letter was dated April 23, 1860, and since the correspondent was in the company of Frederick Brunckow who probably acquired the mine at this time or very shortly thereafter, it is time to meet Brunckow. His biography is found in his file at the Hayden Library. Brunckow was born in 1820 in Berlin, Germany. He was educated at the University of Westphalia and the Royal Mining Academy in Saxony. He joined in a student revolutionary movement in 1848, and upon the failure of the revolution he was forced to flee Germany. According to the celebrated Charles D. Poston, the "Father of Arizona," Brunckow emigrated to New York and fled west, working his way down the Mississippi as a deck hand on a steamboat. In 1856 he was working as a shingle-maker at two-and-a-half-dollars a week and board, when he was asked to join the Sonora Exploring and Mining Company, then outfitting in Texas for a mining venture in Arizona. Needless to say, he accepted with alacrity.

The Sonora Exploring and Mining Company was owned by Poston and Major Samuel P. Heintzelman, once a post commander at Fort Yuma. The outfit arrived in Tucson in August 1856, and set up headquarters south of there at Tubac in the fall. Among the mines the company developed were the "Heintzelman" and "Cerro Colorado," rich in silver, where

Remains of the cabin at the Brunckow Mine. At this site Frederick Brunckow and three others were killed by Mexican miners in 1860. Later, it was the base camp for prospector Ed Schieffelin, who discovered the Tombstone mine.

Brunckow was an assayer and mining engineer. According to Poston, Brunckow was "accomplished in social education, spoke English, German and French fluently...He was a keen sportsman, fond of the chase, and added to his accomplishments the pleasing quality of being an excellent dresser of wild game. The mustang horses frequently formed a favorite dinner at Tubac."

"In 1858," continued Poston, "Brunckow...and other engineers and employees of the company were called to New York to give information about the mines of Arizona, and from realization of the results of their enterprise and hardships were enabled to transfer the festivities of Tubac to Delmonicos, where the pioneers unfolded to the capitalists of Gotham the wonders of the Arizona mines. Brunckow returned to Arizona in 1859 and entered upon the development of the Brunckow mines..."

Thus we trace how Brunckow came into possession of the mine, returning from New York in 1859, visiting the property in April 1860, in company with a correspondent who referred to him as "the distinguished chemist and mineralogist." That he immediately acquired the property, its probable price and another clue to the content of the ore may be concluded from Brunckow's listing in the United States Census of August 28, 1860, where he is shown at the San Pedro Silver Mines, age 40, born in Prussia, occupation mining engineer, property valued at $12,000. From this time on, forever, it would be known as the Brunckow Mine because of the first of the tragic events that had already taken place there, a scant two months before the census date.

In early July 1860, with Brunckow at the mine were three Pennsylvania men, J. C. Moss, brothers William M. and James Williams, a newly-hired German cook, named David Brontrager, and some Mexican peon mine workers, with three or four women and two or three children eleven in all. The shaft was being worked, the kitchen was running, and the store which was standard at all mines had just been stocked with about two thousand dollars worth of merchandise from St. Louis. There was a new steam engine to help work the mine, but it had not been set up. Plenty of arms for defense against Apache raiders were also on hand. So isolated was the mine that the nearest settlement of any kind was the San Pedro Ranch, thirty miles south, in Sonora, Mexico.

A correspondent of a California newspaper supplied the details of the grim story. On Monday, July 23, 1860, William Williams left the mine for Fort Buchanan, thirty-five miles to the west, to purchase flour. Unable to immediately locate a wagon, he was delayed until the 26th to begin his return. With him on the wagon he hired from a Sonoita Valley rancher, Mr. F. G. Acke, were Acke's two boys who were to drive the wagon back. They arrived at a point near the mine very late that night, the team was very tired, and Williams decided to leave the wagon and flour, unharness the team, go on into camp, and return for the wagon in the morning.

Williams and the boys arrived at the mine around midnight, becoming alarmed that something might be wrong when there were no dogs barking at their approach. Nearing the houses, they became aware of a strong stench. They entered the store, could not find a candle, but having two matches struck them for a light. On the floor was the dead body of James Williams. In the dim flare they could see some of the merchandise scattered around on the floor. With no way of knowing who had committed the murder and robbery, or if they were still lurking about, Williams and the boys returned to Fort Buchanan at once for help. Leaving the wagon and flour, they rode the horses back, arriving at the fort about six the next morning.

Captain Ewell immediately sent a Sergeant Henderson with a file of soldiers to look into the matter, find out what had been done and whether by Indians or the Mexican peons, and to follow on their trail. At the mine they found the badly-decayed body of James Williams in the store, the body of Mr. Moss, half-eaten by animals, near the store. Brunckow's body, a long rock drill through it, was found at the bottom of the mine shaft. No trace of Brontrager could be found. All of the Mexicans had disappeared; it was evident that they had murdered the Americans, looted the store, and fled toward Old Mexico. The stench was so great that all of the party was sickened, but "with the help of whiskey and camphor," they gave the murdered men a decent burial. Leaving a few soldiers at the mine and store, Sergeant Henderson and Williams returned to the fort on Sunday, July 29th.

In the meantime, on Friday night, July 27th, about seven p.m., the German cook David Brontrager had stumbled into the camp of the Commission of the Survey of Sonora, badly fatigued and barefooted. He told a hair-raising story of treachery, murder and robbery at the Brunckow Mine. Brontrager had arrived at the mine on Saturday, July 21, to find work. Two days later, Monday morning, William Williams left for the fort. About two or three o'clock that same day two of the peons came into the kitchen, where Brontrager was reading a book, to light their cigars. The peons ranged themselves one on each side of the cook. Suddenly he heard gunshots outside. He tried to go out to find what was happening, but was stopped by the two peons. They told him he must stay there, but that it would be all right with him.

Soon other peons came in and said that the deed was done. They told Brontrager that he was their prisoner and that they would spare his life, as he was known to be a Catholic, had lived some time in Sonora, and none of the peons had anything against him. He had to promise to follow them and not attempt to escape, which he did. After a time he was allowed to look around. In the store was the body of James Williams, a cut on the head, shot several times. Around the corner from the store was the body of Moss, shot twice. Upon inquiring, he learned that they had stabbed Brunckow at the mine shaft and thrown his body into it before surprising the other two. Their object, of course, was plunder.

Immediately the Mexicans began packing their booty on the animals, four of which had belonged to the Americans and three owned by the peons. There was also some money and a little jewelry. Before dark the eleven Mexicans and their prisoner left for Sonora. They traveled thirty miles without stopping, until they reached the San Pedro Ranch, where they released Brontrager. The German cook had wandered, lost in the searing heat of the high desert for three days, until he had stumbled into Camp Jecker, the headquarters of the boundary commission.

A messenger was sent to notify the commanding officer of Fort Buchanan, and Brontrager was sent in a wagon the next morning to the fort for questioning. On the way, he was arrested by the county constable and examined by a "select committee," since there had been some differences in his story. The aroused citizenry was suspicious that, since he had not also been killed, he had been an accessory to the crime. Then he was taken on to the fort, where the commanding officer had him placed in the guardhouse and in irons, to protect him from the angered citizens and hold him as a witness against the peons, once his story had been checked out.

The committee appointed parties of emissaries to cross the line into Sonora to notify the authorities at Santa Clara, Santa Ana, Magdalena, Imuriz and other villages near the line that the murderers if found must be given up. One party of six, mounted and heavily armed, arrived at Santa Cruz before daybreak and surrounded a house occupied by the wife of the peon who had stabbed Brunckow, one Jesus Rodriguez. She and her father were living there, and it was suspected that Rodriguez may have sneaked into the house or was lurking nearby in the town. It was also suspected that the rest of the murderous party had gone on toward Hermosillo. The aid of the prefect of the town of Santa Cruz was sought, and he ordered the house searched. No trace of the murderer was found; the wife insisted that she had not seen him for three months.

The day of this occurrence, August 2nd, a letter was also received at Fort Buchanan from one Durand, commandant of the Santa Cruz military district of Mexico. Durand had gone to Cananea, a copper mining town seventy miles from Santa Cruz, where there was a small military post. There Durand had found that Rodriguez had passed through Cananea the day before and sold some of the plunder from the store at the Brunckow Mine.

Durand confiscated the stolen goods. Rodriguez had told his friends in Cananea that he had killed Brunckow, and his story of the events at the mine were almost the same as that of Brontrager, the cook. At this corroboration of his story, Brontrager was released from custody.

Durand had further stated that he would stay a few days in Cananea to try to capture the murderous crew. Though there were two small military posts, one at the San Pedro Ranch and at Cananea, and though the party had passed through both of them and boasted in both of the deed at the Brunckow mine, no one had attempted to arrest them nor were any of them ever caught or brought to justice. No further comment is needed on Mexican-American relations along the border during this period, only twelve years since the end of war between the two countries, and seven years since the Gadsden Purchase that transferred more Mexican land to the United States.

The Brunckow Mine property was abandoned and remained so for some years. In 1861, the year after Brunckow was killed, the Civil War broke out, the soldiers were called east to fight in that great war, the frontier military posts in Arizona were left unoccupied. The Apache Indians, watching the military withdraw, thought that they had won their battle and stepped up their depredations against the mines and setlements that remained to drive the white man out once and for all. Such was their onslaught that everyone had to flee to such places as Tucson for mutual protection, or out of the territory. During the Civil War most of southern Arizona lay in desolation; there was little movement except in force because of the relentless attacks. The Apache chief, Cochise, and his warriors were completely in command. Even the Sonora Mining Company at Tubac ceased operations, and Charles Poston spent the war in Washington, D.C., trying to get Arizona separated from New Mexico and established as a separate territory. He succeeded, for in 1863 Congress passed the law establishing Arizona Territory separate from that of New Mexico.

These events may seem far removed from our story of the Brunckow Mine, but in fact they are closely connected. President Abraham Lincoln appointed the first territorial officials, who left Washington late in 1863 with a military escort for the new territory. On December 29, 1863, Governor John N. Goodwin and his party reached Navajo Springs in northern

Concrete footings for windlass and mill at an abandoned mine (not the Brunckow) on the Charleston road.

Arizona, a spot which was known to be in the new territory, the flag was run up, and the newly-appointed officials took their oaths of office. One of the men in the party was the first United States Marshal of Arizona, appointed by Lincoln, a man named Milton B. Duffield, who would later figure prominently in the story of the Brunckow Mine. The gubernatorial party traveled to Chino Valley, thence to the new territorial capital, Prescott, to begin their administration.

Arizona from the very beginning has been marked by bitter political rivalries between parties, factions, individuals and sections of the state. In 1866 the state capital was moved by the legislature from Prescott to Tucson, where it remained for ten years. By 1866 the Civil War had ended, the forts were being re-established and soldiers sent back to occupy them to offer settlers, farmers, ranchers and miners some protection from Indian attacks. It would take twenty years to finish the job. It was not until 1872 that Cochise's Apaches made peace and agreed to settle on a reservation with Cochise's friend and blood brother, Tom Jeffords, as agent. That did not stop Apache depredations, which continued for years. In the meantime, new arrivals poured into southern Arizona, settlers, outlaws and fortune hunters of all kinds, many of them embittered southerners adding another faction of hatred to the Arizona political scene.

Through all of this the abandoned Brunckow Mine, its shaft falling in and its buildings deteriorating, baked under the Arizona sun, its three lonely graves testifying to its tragic past. The measure of relief from the Indians afforded by Cochise's treaty in 1872 at last allowed someone to take an interest in the ghostly mine, and it was none other than the former territorial U.S. Marshal, Milton Duffield. Duffield was a controversial figure, a large and powerful man, absolutely fearless, a dead shot, but with a flaming temper, quick on the trigger, querulous and quarrelsome by nature. He resigned as U.S. marshal because he wanted more money than the salary he received, and set out to make his fortune. Constantly in trouble in Tucson for gunplay and threats of it, Duffield relocated and claimed the Brunckow in 1873.

The old buildings were renovated and the mine shafts cleaned out, though Duffield's claim to the property was being disputed by one Joseph T. Holmes. Each claimed that the other had jumped his legitimate property. On June 5, 1874, Duffield rode out to the Brunckow Mine, and entered a house there occupied by Holmes. Holmes seized a double-barreled shotgun and warned Duffield not to come any closer. Unarmed, Duffield continued without a word to advance on Holmes. When he was about fifteen feet away, Holmes let go with both barrels. Some of the pellets struck Duffield in the head, and he fell to the floor and soon was dead. His grave was added to those already on the premises, and Holmes was tried for murder.

Holmes based his defense on Duffield's well-known character of violence, and the first trial ended in a hung jury. He was tried again, and in December was found guilty of manslaughter and sentenced to a stretch in the territorial prison. There was still another development from Duffield's claim when on July 4, 1874, a notice was published by a Mrs. Mary E. Vaughn of Tucson that anyone found on the Brunckow Mine property would be considered a trespasser, since she had bought the property from Duffield the previous year. The county records in Tucson confirmed her claim. Why then Duffield would risk and then even lose his life over the property is a mystery that has never been cleared up.

To that mystery can be added another in the form of a notice, dated January 19, 1874, that "Andrew G. Elliott conveys to O.F. McCarthy and G. H. Oury for $500 one-third interest in the Brunckow lode which contains 1,500 feet and located by Elliott on January 19, 1874." Oury, once mayor of Tucson, was one of the best-known early-day residents of the city. Apparently, however, the claim was again abandoned and again relocated in 1878 by Charles Rodgers, Sidney DeLong and Thomas Jeffords, the latter being the same Jeffords who was the first U.S. agent at the Chiricahua Apache Indian Reservation. By this time the reservation had been abolished, and the Chiricahua Apaches sent to the San Carlos Reservation. Rodgers, DeLong and Jeffords, said the *Arizona Daily Star* on July 15, 1879, "commenced work on (the mine) vigorously. Rodgers was soon after murdered by the Apaches, which caused another suspension of work and added another victim to the list."

Again for a time the mining claim on the remote, sunbaked, wind-swept, alkali hillside overlooking the San Pedro River was uninhabited except for the men who had given their lives for it and slept in the earth near the shaft. But the wild and barren land was on the threshold of a stampede of humanity into it, and a storm of worldwide notoriety such as was seldom, if ever, seen before or since. A few people were filtering in, mostly to locate ranches along the San Pedro, but among them was a prospector named Ed Schieffelin. According to Schieffelin's own story in the files of the Arizona Historical Society, he camped for a time with the would-be ranchers on the river, where they lived together for their mutual protection, while he prospected for minerals in the barren hills by day.

> ...Two men came in from Tucson one night (they had traveled at night on account of the Indians,)" wrote Schieffelin in his account, "who had taken the contract to do the assessment work on the old Brunckow Mine...The next morning they saw me and saw I had a good outfit, a good rifle and plenty of ammunition, and wanted me to stand guard for them while they were at work. I agreed to this, and the next day we went down to the mine. While standing guard I could see the Tombstone Hills very plainly with my field glasses and I took a fancy to them, noticing that there was quite a number of ledges in the neighborhood of the Brunckow Mine, all running in the same direction, about northwest and southeast.
>
> When the two men finished their assessment work on the Brunckow Mine, they started back to some ranches that they had located on the river as they were coming down. On the first day I found some float, and liked the appearance of the country; it was a promising country for mineral...

The rest, as they say, is history, for Schieffelin was the discoverer of the silver mines of fabulous wealth. He named his first claim the "Tombstone," from which the boom town that mushroomed on the mesa near the hills of silver took its name.

Schieffelin's story is well-known. He went to find his brother Al to help him finance and work the claim, for Ed himself was now dead broke. He found Al at the McCracken mine near Signal, where Ed had his ore samples from the Tombstone claim assayed. As a result, the mining engineer at the McCracken, who had assayed Ed's samples, resigned his position to form a partnership with Ed and Al Schieffelin to develop the silver claim on the San Pedro. They left Signal on February 14, 1878, for the Tombstone claim, and set up camp in the abandoned buildings at the Brunckow Mine. The partner, Richard Gird, set up his assay furnace in the fireplace of the old Brunckow cabin, and for the next few months with Al as hunter and cook and Gird as assayer, Ed Schieffelin prospected the nearby hills. By August he had discovered and claimed all of the richest mines ever found there, the Luck Cuss, the Tough Nut, the Contention, and as Ed put it, "We were now satisfied that we had found all we wanted . . ."

They were no longer in lonely isolation, either. The word was out, and soon the hills were swarming with prospectors. Almost every square-inch was covered with mining claims, but none ever equaled the richness of those of Schieffelin and his partners except for the Grand Central, a division of Schieffelin's Contention claim. The dizzying success of the Tombstone mines sparked feverish activity once again at the Brunckow. In the vicinity was a claim called the "Dean Richmond," and another claim near it was called the "Mabel Mine." On April 21, 1881, the *Arizona Daily Star* of Tucson said, "Considerable work is now in progress in the vicinity of the old Brunckow on the Charleston road. Messrs. Donohue and Campbell have a force of men at work on the Mabel, which adjoins the Dean Richmond, and are meeting with encouraging success . . ." On December 3, 1881, the *Weekly Enterprise* of Florence said that a six-foot shaft had been sunk on the Brunckow, which showed a three-foot vein of copper, "which assays $12.57 in silver to the ton, and 58.7 percent copper."

All of this was to be in vain at the Brunckow Mine. The ores proved to be shallow and soon played out, causing work at the mine to cease once again. There were many who remained unconvinced in the frenzy of the early 1880s, and a succession of owners hoping to duplicate the bonanza of Ed Schieffelin and his partners claimed and relocated the Brunckow Mine only to abandon it again. Each time the mine was given up as being, in historian DeVere's words, "absolutely worthless."

It soon wasn't the only "absolutely worthless" mine shaft around. By 1885 the fabulous silver mines near Tombstone were flooding with water. All attempts to pump them out were in vain, the pumps themselves caught fire, the mines filled with water and became absolutely worthless. At least they were "has-beens." The famed Brunckow mine was a "never-was." Everybody associated with it came to grief, heartbreak and tragedy. The Brunckow Mine itself, without Ed Schieffelin's touch of sardonic humor, should have been the true Tombstone Mine.

So if you ever drive from Tombstone to Fort Huachuca on the Charleston Road, pause for a moment near the Brunckow Mine to reflect. But don't disturb the old cabin shell that still stands guard as sort of monument to the stalwarts of long ago, or the old mine shaft near the road. All around you are the ghosts of some of the famous men in Arizona history, like Brunckow, Schieffelin, Poston, Duffield, Earp, Jeffords, Oury. They have all stood where you might stand on the San Pedro hillside, watching in silence the river below, and the sun on the distant mountains.

Remains of adobe building at an abandoned mine (not the Brunckow) on the Charleston road.

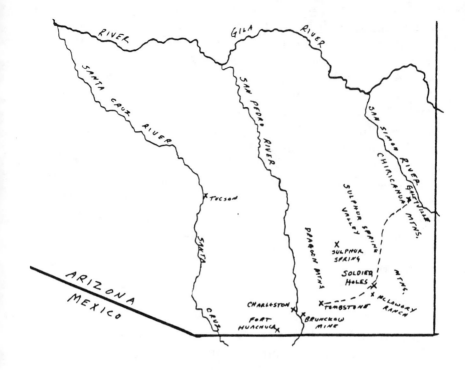

Map for Chapter 10 - Soldier Holes

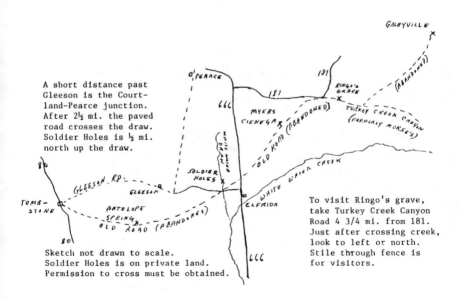

A short distance past Gleeson is the Court-land-Pearce junction. After 2½ mi. the paved road crosses the draw. Soldier Holes is ½ mi. north up the draw.

To visit Ringo's grave, take Turkey Creek Canyon Road 4 3/4 mi. from 181. Just after crossing creek, look to left or north. Stile through fence is for visitors.

Sketch not drawn to scale. Soldier Holes is on private land. Permission to cross must be obtained.

Map for Chapter 10 - Soldier Holes

CHAPTER 10
Soldier Holes

One of the most prominent and frequented spots in Arizona Territory after the Civil War was called Soldier Holes, yet today its location is almost forgotten by even the oldest of residents, even those living close to it. Many of the most famous and notorious people to inhabit Pima and Cochise counties when Tombstone was in its heyday traveled to it or through it, or camped there, including Wyatt Earp and his brothers, Doc Holliday, Sheriffs John Behan and Bob Paul and their deputies, outlaws such as Curly Bill Brocius, John Ringo, Old Man Clanton and his sons, the McLowery brothers, Frank and Tom, killed at the gunfight at the O.K. Corral. Soldier Holes is mentioned and named as a reference point in all of the old accounts of that time.

Soldier Holes' location is on White Water Draw which eventually finds its way to White Water Creek, wandering shallow and often dry in the middle of the great Sulphur Springs Valley. At Soldier Holes pools of water formed on the surface of the ground, rising from Arizona's once-high water table and run-off from rains into the shallow draw. All around were the waist-high stands of nutritious grasses which grew wild, and attracted cattlemen to southern Arizona from as far away as Texas. It was in the heart of the territory of the wild and merciless Chiricahua Apache Indians, who doubtless had used the waterholes for the hundreds of years of their nomadic habitation. It was from the soldiers who watered their horses there while criss-crossing the dry and dusty Sulphur Springs Valley pursuing those same Apaches that the waterholes were named.

In a land where white and red traveler alike depended on life-sustaining waterholes, springs, seeps and wells, it was natural that they should become places where trails and roads converged. People met who would not otherwise meet in a vast wilderness, and there might be strife. Such a place was Soldier Holes. It came to prominence after the discovery by a prospector named Ed Schieffelin of silver lodes in the hills along the San Pedro River, far to the west of Soldier Holes, in 1878. The hills of silver, however rich in minerals, were barren of trees. When the mines opened in 1879 and the town of Tombstone sprang up on the mesa below, there was an immediate and frantic need for lumber, not only to build the town, but for timbers to shore up the vast network of mine tunnels boring through the hills. Timber camps and sawmills were established in the Santa Rita Mountains to the west, the Huachuca Mountains to the southwest, and the Chiricahua Mountains to the east. The road to the latter passed Soldier Holes.

This road ran easterly from Tombstone to Antelope Spring, Soldier Holes, Myers Cienega, with stops at other waterholes and ranches where protection from Apaches could be found, to Morse's Canyon in the Chiricahua Mountains where a man named Morse owned the sawmill. The abundance of water, grasses for forage and good camping sites made Soldier Holes, twenty miles east of Tombstone, a favorite on the fifty-mile trip. Traffic increased on the road in 1881 with the opening of the Texas Mine in the Chiricahua Mountains where the town of Galeyville arose. Tombstone to Galeyville travelers used the road past Soldier Holes to Morse's Canyon, from where a trail led over the mountains to Galeyville.

By some time early in 1880 a man named Sanderson had established a ranch at Soldier Holes. In an unpublished manuscript a deputy sheriff, Billy Breakenridge, mentions riding out to Soldier Holes with Roy Sanderson who was ranching there. The journal of George Parsons, who kept a diary during his years in Tombstone, also mentions Sanderson, who was at Soldier Holes when Parsons camped there with a party on a hunting trip to the Chiricahua Mountains. He was told that it was thirty-five miles to the Morse sawmill by "Sanderson...the proprietor of a well" at Soldier Holes, living there with his family. Parsons notes passing many lumber wagons broken down or having to abandon part of the load. Camped overnight at Soldier Holes, Parsons' party encountered a heavy thunderstorm and used part of the lumber for a rude shelter. He also said that the mosquitos were very bad and that the coyotes howled the whole night through.

A letter in the files of the Arizona Historical Society from Mrs. Mattie S. Chambers, one of the Sanderson children, gives her parents names as William G. and Katherine Lou Sanderson. The family arrived in Arizona on a Colorado River steamer, debarking at Aubrey Landing. They settled on the Gila River near old Fort Thomas, but were forced to move on when the mother contracted malaria from the swarms of mosquitos at the river.

"One fine evening," continues Mrs. Chambers' letter, "we had stopped for the night at some small, round watering places, far in the valley to the south, near the Old Mexico line. Here father was preparing camp and mother was busy with the children and supper, when a cowboy rode into the circle of our firelight. 'Howdy's' were exchanged and the stranger was aksed to 'light and eat.' Soon he was telling father of the awful smallpox epidemic then in Tombstone, which was the nearest town. He said we had better not go near there with all those babies. I can still hear my father as he turned to my mother and said to her, 'Turn out your chickens, Katherine, we will stay here.'

"And so we did. For fifteen years we were happy there in the Sulphur Springs Valley, at the Soldier Hole Ranch. My father brought in the first artesian wells to be found in Arizona, for which the federal government awarded him a thousand dollars... My mother grew stronger there and we prospered in every way. The raiding parties of old Geronimo came by our home many times, plundering and stealing as they went, but never molesting our family."

It was not long until the Sandersons had neighbors, as the reminiscences of the pioneer Brophy family in the Arizona Historical Society tell of the establishment of a ranch at Soldier Holes in 1881. James Brophy, living in Tombstone, camped at Soldier Holes and decided to establish a ranch there. His brother William joined him, and they dug a well, one working at the bottom of the well, the other at the top, operating the lift and keeping sharp watch for the Apaches, rifle in hand. They built a ranch house, which also served meals to travelers and had a bar where liquor could be obtained. Apparently the Brophy brothers did not stay long, selling out to the Chiricahua Cattle Company headquartered further up from the sawmill in Morse's Canyon. James went to work for the cattle company, and William moved on to become a mining official at Bisbee.

Some notorious neighbors also established a ranch about this time, four miles south of Soldier Holes. They were the McLowery brothers, Frank and Tom, who moved from a ranch on Babocamari Creek west of Tombstone. The McLowerys were members of the outlaw confederation under Old Man Clanton, whose real name was Newman Hayes Clanton. It included his sons, Phin, Ike and Billy, Curly Bill Brocius, John Ringo, the Patterson brothers also from the Babocamari country, and dozens of others more or less prominent in the Tombstone saga. The McLowery ranch was the outlaw headquarters for stolen stock in the Sulphur Springs Valley, as were other ranches in the San Pedro and San Simon river valleys. This nefarious business increased the presence of law officers in the valley, at the McLowery Ranch, and at Soldier Holes. When Old Man Clanton was killed by Mexican cowboys, Curly Bill took over leadership of the outlaws with Ringo and Ike Clanton as lieutenants.

Accounts of the events of the day by such eyewitnesses as George Parsons, Billy Breakenridge as deputy under Sheriff John Behan, and by writers such as Walter Noble Burns and Stuart Lake, who interviewed Wyatt Earp and Breakenridge and other pioneers still living at the time of their writing often refer to Soldier Holes. In his memoirs, Breakenridge often mentions the McLowery Ranch and says that outlaws could frequently be seen hanging around Soldier Holes. Sheriff John Behan and his deputies including Breakenridge, it is fair to say after a hundred years' examination of the evidence, were in cahoots with and the political allies of the outlaws individually and as a gang. Some of this evidence is made plain in a series of interviews with Breakenridge in 1926 by representatives of the Arizona Historical society, transcripts of which are preserved in the Society's files. One of these interviews follows in its entirety, in Breakenridge's own words to preserve its original flavor and integrity, since the incident described has appeared in other publications in drastically altered form. It concerns the recovery of a stolen horse belonging to E. B. Gage, wealthy owner of one of the Tombstone mines.

"Well, now, getting the horse," recounts Breakenridge. "Well, it seems that Sherman McMasters had been arrested for something by—I think it was by Virg Earp. But afterward he was turned loose from the jail at night. Later on he left the country with the Earps. Well, after he got loose he went up Contention Hill and stole the saddle horse belonging to E. B. Gage. He went over in the valley and he traded him to one of the Hicks boys—Milt Hicks. In the meantime one of the cowboys that lived down the San Pedro rode into town—Phin Clanton, quite a good friend of mine. He met me on the street and says 'If you want that Contention horse, if you get to McLowery's ranch before dark you will find him there.'

"I got out a John Doe warrant. My horse was pretty well played out—I had just got in from a trip—so I went down to the stable and got a little gray pony. Slow as mud, I found out. I couldn't even lead him along fast enough to get to McLowery's before dark. It rained on me on the way, but it cleared up and was moonlight when I got there. There was no horse in the corral.

"Knowing that some of the gang was likely to be there, I thought I'd better let 'em know who I was, so I hollered. Frank McLowery come out and I told him who it was, and when he opened the door I see that his house was full of cowboys. And so when I got off my horse why I told Frank I wanted to see him a minute and we walked around the corner and I told him I was after the Contention horse, and 'I have got to get him. You fellows are taxpayers and you dasn't let me go back without the horse as it would look bad.' He says 'The horse ain't here now, but I'll see what I can do.' But as soon as he went in he spoke to Milt Hicks, and they went out and it didn't take but a minute to have it spread among the gang there who I was and what I was after. Curly Bill was there, and as he was a pretty good friend of mine we joked about it.

"'How are you going to take the horse?' one of them asked. 'I'll take him all right. Just now the trouble is to find him.' So Frank come in pretty soon and told me 'I think the horse will be here in the morning.' So we all laid down and went to sleep. The next morning this Frank McLowery was the first one up and as he went out to build a fire I was up too, and the whole gang got up at the same time. Curly says 'I'll go out and help you catch the horse' just as though I didn't know how to handle a rope, though of course I wasn't as good at it as some of them maybe.

"On the way out he says 'The boys are pretty hot about this, and they don't dare do anything here, but when you get away, look out, for they're going to take him away from you.' You see, the gang there wasn't employed by McLowery's or any one, but was just regular rustlers. They made the place their rendezvous. When I got ready to go I knew how hard it was to lead my pony, so I says to myself 'I'll just ride him and lead the Contention horse.' Just as I started out I saw five of the gang there come down from Soldier Holes and away they went up towards Tombstone, up through the pass. They didn't follow me, but went ahead, and after what Frank had told me I knew they was going to stop me somewhere and try to get the horse back.

"I couldn't figure out just where they'd catch me, unless it would at at Antelope Springs. The road into Tombstone went through by the Springs then, and from there you could see for miles down the valley. When I went over to the wagon road there was a fellow camped there with two wagons finishing his breakfast, and just getting ready to pull out, so then I seen my only chance and says 'Don't start up—just wait a minute.' So I asked him to lead the gray pony into Tombstone, and I throwed the saddle on the Contention horse. Once I'd done that I felt happy, because I knowed they couldn't catch me then. He was a spirited horse, and pretty fast.

"I see them coming across the valley, making for Antelope Springs, but still a mile or more away, so I took a short cut for Tombstone straight up through the pass and off the wagon road, and they veered off and come after me, but they didn't never get within half a mile of me. They fired two or three shots, but whether they was shooting at me

I don't know. I didn't hear the bullets whistle. So I rode up to the Contention Mine and turned the horse over.

"I saw most of that bunch a week or so later, and they just laughed about what had happened. Thought I'd played it pretty slick. We was always friends in spite of anything that come up. No, I was never scared. I always felt so much confidence in them fellows. I knew they wouldn't kill me if they didn't have to. If I'd a went to arrest one of them for any serious crime they'd a made a serious fight. But Lord, cattle and horse stealing wasn't no serious crime then. They could always prove a dozen alibis that they was some place else a hundred miles away when the stock was stole. That didn't bother them none."

Another of the interviews with Breakenridge and George Parsons' journal both recount an instance when a Tombstone posse took up the trail of raiding Apaches, in which Soldier Holes figured prominently. This incident occurred early in October 1881, only three weeks before the gunfight at the O.K. Corral. Late in September a band of a hundred renegade Chiricahua Apaches under Geronimo and Sanchez had broken out of the San Carlos reservation on the warpath. On October 2nd at Cedar Springs fifteen miles northwest of Fort Grant they attacked Samaniego's freight wagon train, killing Samaniego's brother and five teamsters.

On October 5th the Apaches had engaged in a running fight with troops pursuing them, and the band broke into smaller groups heading for Old Mexico, raiding as they went. Part of them continued down the eastern slopes of the Dragoon Mountains, and part had gone through the middle pass of the Dragoons a short distance from the Cochise Stronghold. While traveling on county business, Breakenridge had stopped for the night at Persley and Woolf's ranch near Sulphur Spring, and the next morning in the company of Woolf, Breakenridge had started for Tombstone by way of this middle pass of the Dragoons. Entering it they found tracks of about twenty Indians who had preceded them, and on the other side of the pass found where they had stampeded a team hauling wood. The wagon was broken down and the animals, from which the harness had been stripped, had been driven away. A hundred yards further was the body of the teamster, his head smashed in by rocks.

Breakenridge and Woolf hurried to Tombstone, where they reported what they had seen, and a party went out to bring in the body of the murdered man. In the meantime, the Apaches who had murdered him hastened toward Mexico in the direction of

Antelope Spring, eleven miles east of Tombstone. The main body of the Apaches had hurried toward Mexico on a more easterly route, and the soldiers following them had gone into camp at Soldier Holes to wait for their supply mules to catch up.

A call went out in Tombstone for volunteers for a posse to help fight the Apache raiders. Breakenridge lists the volunteers besides himself as Sheriff John Behan, Wyatt and Virgil Earp, then Tombstone city marshal, John P. Clum, then mayor, Ward Priest, Charles Reppy, Frank Ingoldsby, George Parsons, Marshall Williams, Cy Bryant, and a dozen nameless others; Parsons incidentally mentions one "Mills." At the edge of town they stopped to organize; Behan was elected captain and Virgil Earp lieutenant. The posse hastened to Antelope Spring where they found the trail of the Indians heading for the McLowery ranch south of Soldier Holes.

Just at the time the trail was found it began to rain heavily. Soon all the men were soaked, and in the lower spots it became boggy and made slow going for the horses. The posse pressed on to Frink's ranch, two miles south of the McLowery ranch. Here Frink gave them hot coffee, and told them the Indians had run off all his stock except one horse, and some twenty-seven head of stock from the McLowery ranch. They were headed south toward the Swisshelm Mountains. The men of the posse tried to sleep in the cabin out of the heavy rain, but it was very small, and they slept very wet and cold every which way on the floor and the bare furniture.

At three in the morning the rain had stopped and the moon came out. The posse mounted up and pursued the Apaches by moonlight, horses floundering in the muddy going. At Horseshoe Pass, now known as Leslie Canyon in the Swisshelm Mountains, they found the trail of Indians and stopped to take counsel. It was now dawn, and the skies had cleared. Breakenridge and Frink were designated to scout up the pass for signs of Indians while the rest of the posse waited. Breakenridge went up one side of the pass and Frink the other. Frink signaled Breakenridge that he had found where the Indians had gone over a low divide that morning. From a hill they spotted them, fifteen braves a mile ahead, followed by some squaws driving the stolen stock.

The scouts hurried back to the main group, to find that it had left in the direction of the McLowery ranch. Breakenridge followed the posse to the ranch, where he found it cooking breakfast. Frink followed the Indians alone, and managed to get between the Apaches and the stock, then stampede part of the animals back toward his ranch. The Apaches were so pressed to escape the troops that they did not even pursue Frink, but hurried on toward Mexico. Frink returned to the McLowery ranch to inform the posse that the Indians he saw were a few stragglers, and the main body had already passed on ahead.

While the posse was still at the McLowery ranch, a notorious outlaw den, Curley Bill and two of his younger followers arrived. It is interesting to note the presence all at one time of the sheriff, his deputy Breakenridge, Wyatt and Virgil Earp, a federal marshal and city marshal, the chief of the outlaws, Curly Bill and several of his gang at one of their hideouts.

Curly Bill having brought word that the soldiers were camped at Soldier Holes, four miles away, the posse took counsel again. It decided to go there to report to the commander, Col. Reuben Bernard, and offer its services to the military. At Soldier Holes the posse found the soldiers still in camp, waiting for supplies and resting their weary horses. One company of soldiers was the famous "Buffalo Soldiers," whom Parsons noted had acquitted themselves well when fighting Indians the day before. Also in camp were several Apache scouts attached to Bernard's command, who knew John Clum well from his days as Apache agent at San Carlos. Clum and the scouts greeted each other warmly and talked long about his days among the Apaches at the reservation.

The men of the posse found that a wagonload of supplies, food and drink and even liquor, had been sent out from Tombstone for their use. Some of them went on back to town, but the rest stayed in camp, making good use of the supplies. That night they also made good use of the liquor. The next morning Colonel Bernard told the Tombstone men, with thanks for their offer of service, that he was sure his men could handle the situation, and started off after the Indians. Parsons' report of this is scornful. "The command took up the trail toward the Chiricahuas this a.m. and moved leisurely off, bugles blowing an hour beforehand so as to notify all Indians to get out of the way. They could be seen and heard miles away by Indians. This is no way to fight them at all," he sniffed. The posse returned to Tombstone and a warm welcome, finding that false rumors of a fight with the Indians in which Clum was said to have been wounded had preceded them.

The memoirs of Joseph "Mack" Axford, longtime range boss of the cattle ranch of W. C. Greene, cattle and copper baron of southern Arizona in the late 1800s and early 1900s, mention an incident at Soldier Holes involving outlaws and another of Tombstone's legendary characters, Buckskin Frank Leslie. Axford attributes the tale to one Joe Tasker, who must have owned the bar at Soldier Holes at one time. Leslie had been a soldier and scout for the military, but during his years at Tombstone usually occupied his time as a gambler and bartender at the Oriental Saloon, where Wyatt Earp had a partnership in the gambling concession. As a gunman Leslie was considered top drawer, one of the quickest and deadliest, with whom other gunmen avoided confrontation. At times he was included in posses because of his abilities as a tracker.

Leslie also had a ranch he was trying to build up on the east slope of the Swisshelm Mountains southeast of Tombstone, and Soldier Holes was about halfway between them. Leslie often stopped at Soldier Holes for drinks and meals, and of course was well acquainted with the outlaws who had many drinking bouts there. On one occasion Buckskin Frank's horse became lame, and he had to stay overnight to rest it. During the afternoon Frank and Joe Tasker got to experimenting with mixing drinks, which of course had to be sampled. The effect to be expected on such experimenters was the result. At about four in the afternoon a bunch of outlaws rode in fast from the direction of Mexico, with Russian Bill in the lead. As they pulled up in a cloud of dust, Russian Bill hollered: "I'm Russian Bill, a wolf with a red eye and it's my day to howl!"

There was bad blood already between Russian Bill and Buckskin Frank over the affections of a red-light girl in Tombstone. Bill entered the Soldier Holes saloon with the rest of the gang piling in behind him, when he was brought up short by the cutting voice of Leslie. "Bill, how much money have you got on you?" asked Frank. Russian Bill recognized the challenge in Leslie's voice, and his answer was deliberate. "About eighty, Frank," he said. "Put it on the bar," Leslie told him, and Russian Bill did as he was told. Leslie waved the rest of the outlaws up to the bar. "Drink it up, boys, it's Bill's day to howl," he told them. Axford commented that this was a tough challenge in front of Russian Bill's friends and undoubtedly hard to take. Both of the participants in this little exchange came to bad ends. Russian Bill was lynched in New Mexico for stealing a horse, and Leslie spent several years in Yuma Prison for killing a woman at his ranch.

Soldier Holes was also one of the last places visited by the widely notorious outlaw John Ringo, according to some published accounts, before he rode away to a mysterious death. Ringo had been on a prolonged drinking spree that started in Tombstone with Buckskin Frank Leslie and Billy Claiborne, an outlaw hanger-on, as his companions, late in July 1882. He rode out of Tombstone toward Galeyville with Leslie and Clairborne following, and they continued their binge in the bars along the road at Antelope Spring, Soldier Holes and Myers Cienega. Ringo rode away alone one morning toward Galeyville, with Leslie soon following, and Clairborne lost to the story. The next day some lumber haulers found Ringo dead, sitting on a flat rock in a grove of live oak trees in Morse's Canyon, shot through the head. A hastily-organized coroner's jury gave a verdict of suicide, but close examination of the evidence reveals that it almost certainly was not. Though Ringo's six-gun was found in his hand, there were five cartridges in it and the hammer went down on an empty chamber as was the custom then. Ringo's rifle, leaning against a nearby tree, had an unfired cartridge in the breech. There were no burnt powder marks where the bullet entered. Ringo's horse and boots were missing, the horse later found with the boots attached to the pommel of the saddle; the outlaw's feet were wrapped in strips torn from his undershirt. For one reason or another various people were rumored to have murdered him. In November Billy Claiborne announced that he was going to kill Frank Leslie for murdering Ringo. When friends told Leslie that Claiborne was waiting outside for him with a rifle, Frank stepped out the side door of the Oriental and called to Billy. As Claiborne whirled to meet him, Leslie shot his man dead with a bullet in the chest.

Such was life in Arizona Territory when Soldier Holes was a prominent and popular location. Doubtless it was visited many times early in 1882 by Wyatt Earp's federal posse while trailing outlaws under orders from Arizona Governor Tritle and U.S. Marshal C. P. Dake, before Earp left Arizona in May of that year never to return. After the earthquake of 1887 the water in the waterholes and artesian wells no longer flowed as freely, though some remained. The new railroad twenty-five miles to the north took much of the traffic that once made its waypast Soldier Holes, and when late in the 1880s and early 1890s the mines in Tombstone were closing, the need for timbers ceased. The sawmill closed, and by that time Galeyville had long been a ghost town. Travel on the old road past Soldier Holes became a trickle.

Because new mines were opening in the vicinity, however, the water supply at Soldier Holes made it desirable, for the location of an ore mill.

With the employees of the mill settling around it, Soldier Holes at last had enough inhabitants to apply to the government for its own post office. They got it, all right, but to their horror not under the name of "Soldier Holes," but as "Descanso!" An 1892 issue of the *Arizona Weekly Enterprise* told how it came about:

"A petition was sent in asking for a postmaster and the establishment of a post office at Soldier Holes. The petition was duly received at Washington, and the assistant postmaster general, whose duty it was to look after mushroom towns in the West, was staggered at the name which the inhabitants called their town.

"He carried it to Wannamaker, who took it to Mrs. Harrison, and each one decided there was no mistake about it. It read "Soldier Holes" and no one could make it out differently. What to do about it (!) was the next question. Mark Smith (Marcus Aurelius Smith, brilliant attorney then the representative of Arizona Territory to Congress) was summoned and asked to interpret the name of the proposed United States mail depository in Cochise County. "Why, that's easy enough," said Marcus (who once had practiced in Tombstone), "the place was designated as "Soldier Holes" for the reason that there were water holes there years before any settlers appeared in that section, where the soldiers watered their horses or often camped while on a hot trail of Apache renegades.

"The explanation was quickly laid before Mr. Wannamaker who in turn carried the news to Mrs. Harrison, who seized the Spanish dictionary, which had been laid aside after the Mexican minister had retired a few minutes before, and after turning the pages over, wrote on a slip of paper "Descanso, a haven of rest."

And thus was the lively infant brought into the vocabulary of Uncle Sam's post office service." "Descanso" didn't last long, though. The post office was discontinued in 1894, and a 1904 map of Cochise County showed the location as "Soldier Holes" again.

Maps for Chapter 11 - Adamsville

From Florence take the Adamsville Road west. It is not
quite four miles on the speed-
ometer. After about 1½ miles
Butte View Cemetery is just off
the right side of the road.
About two miles further, on
the right-hand side where the
road turns left up the rise
to the Coolidge highway, is
a collection of farm buildings,
some of them vacant. In the
fields beyond was the site
of Adamsville.

Sketch not drawn to scale.

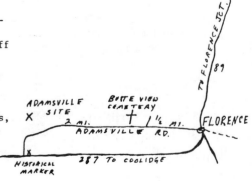

CHAPTER 11
Adamsville, A.T.

This narrative of Arizona's once prominent but now obscure places has purposefully skirted its many fascinating ghost towns, but there is an exception. That is the story of old Adamsville, its history buried in bits and pieces in old newspaper files, manuscripts in the files of historical societies, and occasionally mentioned in books. Stitched together, these bits and pieces reveal the saga of a town as wild and woolly as almost any the territory ever held, of men famous and infamous who came to and went from it, and an interplay between these men and the incidents that befell them that form a crazy quilt pattern as rich in Old West history as any ghost town in Arizona Territory.

Adamsville's story began in 1866, the year after the end of the Civil War, when Charles S. Adams filed his declaration statement on June 15 on a tract of land in the Gila River bottom four miles from what is now Florence, dug an irrigation ditch, and began his farm. In that same year, the first house was built in Florence, and the new Indian agent there, Levi Ruggles, laid out the town and began offering lots. Down the river at his location Adams laid out a townsite, too, and began giving away lots to anyone who would build on them. Naturally for free lots there were more takers, and Adamsville got off to a fast start. Adams' neighbors named the town for him and started building with all due speed.

Charles Adams' free lot strategy paid off in other ways, because he promptly built a store and saloon on the best lots which he had reserved for that purpose. These establishments were, of course, well patronized, and Adams was on his way to becoming a successful merchant in his own town. Down the road a few miles on the Gila River Indian Reservtion at the village of Blackwater an astute man, William Bichard, and his brother Nick were running the first trading post there with the Pima Indians. They knew a good thing when they saw it, and took up some lots in Adamsville upon which they also built some business establishments. When trader Ammi White, who had a trading post and flour mill on the reservation at Casa Blanca, decided to sell out, the Bichard brothers bought the flour mill and moved it to Adamsville. White's mill had been the only one between Tucson and California, and he had done a large business with the military. Bichard inherited the contracts to furnish flour and barley to the military establishments.

In 1868 the Gila River overflowed in one of its periodic spring floods, destroying the flour mill. Bichard had a new one, with all of the latest improvements, shipped in at great expense from the Pacific coast, erected it at Adamsville in 1869, and was back in the milling business. Before leaving the subject of Bichard and his mills, it should be noted that he erected the first flour mill in Phoenix, on the block where the Luhrs building now stands, and, according to the *Arizona Miner*, "On July 4, 1871, the Bichard Flouring Mill steamed up and made the first flour ever ground in the Salt River Valley." This occurred some months before the Hellings Mill in east Phoenix and the Hayden Mill in Tempe began operations. Unfortunately, after only three months, the Bichards' Phoenix Mill burned down with a loss of $10,000, and was never rebuilt.

Adamsville never had the distinction of having a newspaper, something most new towns boasted within a short time after being founded. The *Weekly Arizonan* of Tucson carried this advertisement on January 22, 1870: "Adamsville Saloon! Charles Adams, Main Street, Adamsville. This pioneer establishment keeps first class accommodations and every class of refreshments." Charles Adams was not destined to enjoy for long life in the town he had founded and bore his name. Sometime in 1870 or 1871 all his property and interests were purchased by the Bichard brothers, and Adams went to work for them.

The *Arizona Weekly Miner* on September 23, 1871, reported that "Charles S. Adams is now the agent for W. Bichard and Co. in Prescott. The establishment is on the corner of Granite and Gurley Streets in the building formerly occupied by Henderson and Bro." Less than two months later, Adams was dead, killed on November 5th in one of the most famous incidents in Arizona history, the "Wickenburg Massacre." Adams had a wife and three small children in San Francisco, and started for that city to bring them back to Prescott. Just west of Wickenburg, bound for Ehrenberg on the Colorado River, the stagecoach was attacked by renegade Indians from the nearby Date Creek Reservation. Only two of the seven passengers survived, and

Adams was cut down while running for the protection of some rocks.

With the departure of Adams, William Bichard became the dominant figure in the town of Adamsville. He owned a large farming operation, the flour mill, stores, a saloon and other properties obtained from Adams. With his brother and partner Nick, two other Bichards were shown on the census, Stephen and Elias. In 1870 William was 29 years of age, listed as a retail merchant with property worth sixty thousand dollars. That same year he was appointed Inspector of Elections at the precinct that headquartered at the Bichard Trading Post in the Pima village of Blackwater.

Though he was reputed to have been the first trader on the Pima Reservation, and apparently the Indians were satisfied since he bought tons of their wheat for his mill, all was not sweetness and light with the government's licensing authorities. In his report on August 18, 1871, Special Agent J. S. Stout stated that though Bichard had a trading post for several years, his last application for a license had been refused by Stout's predecessor, Capt. F. E. Grossman, because Grossman considered Bichard untrustworthy in this capacity. Bichard continued to operate without a license until Grossman seized his trading post on June 20, 1871. But a month later, on July 24th, Grossman was relieved. In his report to Supt. Herman Bendell on August 16, 1871, Grossman said that Bichard ceased operations when seized, but two other illicit traders, F. M. Larkin and H. Morgan and Co. (see chapter on Morgan's Ferry) continued to oppose the law, and Bichard had opened up again at Blackwater. Grossman complained that enforcement of the law was made difficult because the territorial governors and other officials sided with the "illicit" traders. It may have been that personal vendettas were involved here, as often happened in early Arizona.

In 1871 a post office was established at Adamsville with William Dupont as the postmaster. McCormick, now the territorial delegate in Washington, D.C., had a personal grudge against Charles Adams, and used his influence to get the post office department to change the name of Adamsville to Sanford, in honor of Capt. George B. Sanford. The captain was once Arizona's most famous Indian fighter, stationed at Fort McDowell, but by this time had been transferred. McCormick obviously hoped that by substituting this famous name the town would forget Adams, but he was wrong. The people living there went on calling their town "Adamsville," and others, highly incensed at McCormick's duplicity, urged writers to the town to use the address, "Sanford P.O., Adamsville, A.T." Dupont was succeeded as postmaster by Larkin W. Carr, and in 1872 by William Bichard himself.

During these years, and accelerating in the early 1870s, a rift between two factions in Adamsville and its vicinity had been slowly building until a blood feud finally burst out. On one side were American settlers, and on the other mostly Mexican residents and transient workers. Unexplained killings and disappearances of Americans resulted in deep suspicion of the Mexicans and the forming of an American vigilante group. These suspicions became inflamed with the killing of the highly-respected Baker family by Mexicans at Blue Water Station (see Butterfield Trail chapter) early in 1872. When in March of that year a William McFarland disappeared, the vigilantes were aroused to white-hot anger.

These activities were reported in the Tucson *Citizen*, a newspaper in the seat of Pima County in which Adamsville and Florence were located, Pinal County not being formed until 1875. McFarland had left his home in Sacaton, visited in Adamsville and Florence, and stopped at the house of Pancho Gandara near Blackwater, ten miles from Adamsville. He was never seen again. The vigilantes decided it was time for them to go into action. A $1,200 reward was offered for information concerning McFarland's disappearance, and two weeks went by as the search continued. The vigilantes then advanced in force on the Gandara house, according to their story to get at the truth. One James Bodel and another man started to go inside the house, when Gandara suddenly pulled a gun and killed Bodel. Gandara was himself immediately shot to death by the vigilantes. The battle between the two factions was on.

The vigilantes returned to Adamsville, looking for an alleged Mexican bad man named Manuel Reyes. In the bloodthirsty atmosphere other shootings occurred, a young Mexican named Aguilar was killed and a white man named Perry was shot from his horse. Reyes swore that he would kill four Americans to avenge the death of Gandara, but early the next day he was forced to hole up in a house belonging to one D. C. Thompson, and was surrounded. Some women in the house were allowed out, then the house was blown up. Reyes came out shooting, and was killed.

It is interesting to note that this apparently occurred with the territorial governor, and a detachment of troops also, in town and perhaps watching the incident. After the shootings of Bodel and Gandara, which happened on a Saturday, messages had been sent to Fort McDowell and to the towns of Pinal City and Tucson for assistance. The messenger to Tucson went by way of the stage station in Picacho Pass, where Governor Safford had stopped for the night with his escort of Colonel Morrow and fifteen men. A Sergeant Bruckett with a detachment of twenty-one men from Fort McDowell had also stopped there. Morrow volunteered to take his men to Adamsville, Governor Safford persuaded Bruckett to take his men there, and they were all in Adamsville early Sunday, the day Reyes was killed.

The newspaper reported that the governor used all of his powers of persuasion to talk the vigilantes out of taking the law into their own hands, but they were determined that Reyes should die. Safford promised to have the "bad men" arrested and brought to trial, all to no avail. Colonel Morrow also joined in the governor's pleas, and the newspaper congratulated Morrow and Sergeant Bruckett on their "excellent conduct." Apparently no force or anything beyond persuasion was used to stop the vigilantes from getting Reyes, nor was anyone arrested in connection with his death. His killing, however, seemed to calm the atmosphere for the time being.

War broke out again in Adamsville in November of the same year, when the Tucson *Citizen* reported more killings. After a heated argument in a saloon, Captain Henry Kennedy invited John Rodgers to meet him outside, and they retired to the saloon's back yard. Those inside heard shots, rushed out, and found that Rodgers was still standing but Kennedy lay dead, shot through, an empty gun on the ground beside him and a loaded gun in his pocket. At Rodgers hearing before a judge, Robert L. Swope and H. Bledsoe testified that they had seen the whole thing and that Rodgers had fired in self-defense. Rodgers was then freed, and a coroner's jury found that Kennedy had been shot to death by Rodgers while he was acting in self-defense.

The very next day Robert Swope, the same man who had testified at Rodgers' hearing, was shot and killed at the same saloon in Adamsville. At the coroner's inquest testimony was to the effect that John Willis had killed Swope seemingly without any reason, and that Swope was unarmed. The verdict of the coroner's jury was that Swope had met death from a gunshot fired by Willis, who was then questioned by the judge, but for some reason released from custody. For what reason and why it did not again arouse the vigilantes the newspaper did not speculate. Willis went to Tucson a few days later and was, to his surprise, immediately arrested by Sheriff Ott on a warrant issued by District Judge Titus and jailed. He seemed to think that his discharge after his preliminary hearing would be the end of the matter. The judge, however, expressed his determination to stop the business of murder in his district, and the people of Adamsville agreed in the arrest and jailing of Willis.

The *Citizen* this time did speculate that Willis would eventually be let off again, adding that there was talk in Tucson among some "pretty good men" that maybe they ought to have a Vigilance Committee to see that the punishment prescribed by law for the "terrible crime of murder" should be administered. "Murder upon murder," said the *Citizen,* "is committed in Arizona, yet not one murderer has ever been punished as the law directs." Willis, however, was indicted and brought to trial the following May. Found guilty, he was brought before Judge Titus for sentencing. When asked if he had anything to say before sentence was passed, Willis replied that he did not think he had a fair trial. The judge thought otherwise and sentenced him to hang, but did not set a date for the execution. Willis' attorney promptly appealed to the Supreme Court, which would not meet until the next January.

Fate then took a hand in the case of John Willis. In August a Tucson man and his wife were murdered in their own house while they slept. Three men promptly were arrested and jailed for the crime, and one confessed that the three had committed the acts of which they were accused, murder and robbing the house. The citizens of Tucson waited until the couple's funeral was over, then several hundred assembled in front of the city jail. Two heavy posts were implanted in the ground, and a stout pole about twelve feet long placed on them. Four nooses were fastened to it, and two wagons drawn beneath them. A Catholic priest was allowed in the jail to give such comfort as he could to the men in the jail. When he was finished, the three and Willis were brought out of the jail with black bandages over their eyes. They were put into the wagons, the nooses adjusted, the wagons driven away, and the men hanged side by side.

The *Citizen* reported on the inquest over the bodies of the four men:

"We, the undersigned, the jurors summoned to appear before Solomon Warner, the coroner...to inquire into the cause of the deaths...that they came to their deaths in the courthouse plaza, in the town of Tucson, by hanging; and we further find that the said hanging was committed by the people of Tucson, en masse; and we do further say that in view of the terrible and bloody murders that had been committed by the three, and the tardiness with which justice was being meted out to John Willis, a murderer, that the extreme measures taken by our fellow citizens this morning in vindication of their lives, their property, and the peace and good order of society, while it is to be regretted and deplored that such extreme measures were necessary, seems to the jury to have been the inevitable results of allowing criminals to escape the penalties of their crimes."

It is doubtful that lawlessness was much abated in Adamsville, then at its peak with a reputation as one of the wildest, toughest towns in the territory. In 1870 the census listed it with 400 residents and 160 houses. According to a monograph in the Pinal County Historical Museum in Florence, "Miners from the hills, farmers along the river, soldiers and aventurers, tamed and untamed, made Adamsville their headquarters. It was indeed a popular and thriving village. It was from Adamsville that Pima and Papago Indians left on the morning of December 18, 1872, for a ride into the Pinals to recapture ten horses taken from them by the Apaches. They were successful, and returned with their horses, two captives, some trinkets, and twenty-five dollars in greenbacks."

However, early in 1873 Adamsville suffered a blow from which it seemed never to recover. Its wealthiest and most prominent citizen, its steadying influence and shrewdest businesman, William Bichard, contracted acute bronchitis and died on the first of February. Control of the Bichards' operations fell upon his brother Nick, who never exhibited the strength and acumen of William, and the company was soon in decline. It is possible that Nick Bichard sought the assistance of one of the most respected of Arizona pioneers, Mr. Emerson O. Stratton, much sought because of his reputation as a top-notch accountant, something rare in Arizona territory. Stratton moved to Adamsville, but stayed only a year. His memoirs are to be found in the files of the Arizona Historical Society.

"When I quit my job in Florence," wrote Mr. Stratton, "I moved my family...downriver to Adamsville...(The Bichards had) established a flour mill in Adamsville, to grind the wheat brought in by the Indians...They even shipped grain and flour to Prescott, bringing back lumber and merchandise with which they would establish quite a trading post...The store and mill were on the same side of the one and only street in Adamsville, and right next to the Buckalew and Ochoa store. Oscar Buckalew and Jose Ochoa were both from Florence, but Jose was often confused with his famous uncle of the same name in Tucson. They had a large trade with the Mexicans, and also conducted a large freighting operation.

"I moved my family into quarters provided by Nick Bichard—two rooms of a long, narrow, six-room house. Our quarters were very comfortable and had wooden floors, a big inducement to Carrie to move to Adamsville. Next to us was a saloon, and next to that was the butcher shop. The butcher had his own herd of cattle, and when he killed he would strip out the tenderloin in one long chunk and sell it to us at the same price as any other part of the animal. Imported merchandise was high, not only in Adamsville but in Florence as well, because freight from Yuma was ten cents a pound. But at least meat and flour were cheap."

Stratton's moving his family back to Florence after a year was symbolic of the condition of Adamsville. With the drop in the Bichards' fortunes, the whole town began to decline. Symptomatic of Adamsville's slow death was the discontinuance of the post office in 1876. For fifty years the little town held on before succumbing. "With Florence growing up to the east less than four miles away," continues the monograph in the Pinal county Historical Museum, "and the advent of the railroad...the settlers moved away...By 1920 Adamsville had become merely a dilapidated row of roofless houses."

So old Adamsville may be gone, but it is not forgotten, principally because of the citizens of the town that was its rival and the cause of its demise, Florence. Recently the old Adamsville cemetery, now known as "Butte View Cemetery" though there once were two adjoining cemeteries, was rediscovered. The Pinal County Historical Society has lovingly restored the neglected and vandalized old cemetery.

Adamsville's own tombstone is found at the end of the Florence-Adamsville road, a highway marker at the intersection of the Coolidge highway. The epitaph reads: "The Ghost Town of Adamsville—in the 1870s a flour mill and a few stores formed the hub of life in Adamsville, where shootings and knifings were commonplace, and life was one of the cheapest commodities. Most of the adobe houses have been washed away by the flooding Gila River."

CHAPTER 12
Fort Moroni

Thousands of people every year turn north from Flagstaff's main street, Santa Fe Avenue, on U.S. Highway 180 right in the business district. They are vacationers bound for the Grand Canyon, or Arizonans headed for the Snow Bowl ski area in winter. They pass shopping centers and homes, pass the Museum of Northern Arizona, roll through the foothills with the grandeur of the San Francisco Peaks as a backdrop through what were picturesque ranch properties, but now are sub-divisions. A few miles along the Snow Bowl road turns off at the edge of a large, once-beautiful valley through which Highway 180 continues, now dotted with homes. A great minority know that this is Fort Valley, once known as Leroux Prairie and that in the middle of it stood the structures of Fort Moroni.

In the years just after the Civil War, northern Arizona was a vast, almost unknown area inhabited largely by Indians and with but few white people. There were a few Mormon settlements springing up, mostly along the Little Colorado River, and there were a few Indian trading posts. The catalyst for the settlement of this huge area with its lovely, lonely scenery was the building of the transcontinental railroad connecting the burgeoning new state of California with the populous east. Construction crews of the railroad building westward established work camps at sites which later became the cities of Holbrook, Winslow and Flagstaff. The camp at Flagstaff had about twenty frame buildings and the same number of tents.

In an article in *Plateau* magazine, the publication of the Northern Arizona Society for Science and Art, Mr. Roger E. Kelly described the circumstances leading to the building of Fort Moroni. John W. Young, a son of Mormon leader Brigham Young, and Ammon M. Tenney obtained a contract with the Atlantic and Pacific Railroad Company for grading the right-of-way and building the roadbed, and for furnishing fifty thousand railroad ties. In the spring of 1881 Young and his Mormon workers set up two camps in the Flagstaff area, one near the present business district and the other in what was then known as Leroux Prairie near the famous Leroux Spring, both named for the legendary mountain man and guide, Anton

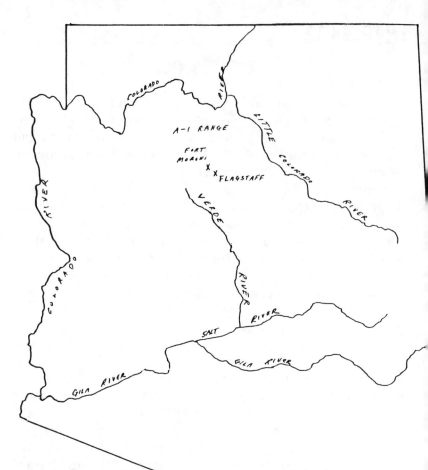

Map showing location
of Fort Moroni

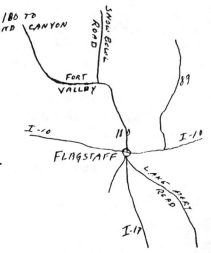

Sketch not drawn to
scale. Take Hwy. 180
north from Flagstaff
toward Grand Canyon.
In a few miles 180 has
a junction with the road
to the Snow Bowl. Continuing
westerly from this junction
Hwy. 180 immediately crosses
Fort Valley. In the middle of
the valley to the south of the
road stood Fort Moroni/Rickerson.
There are no longer any remains.

Leroux. This area came to be called Fort Valley because of the building there of Fort Moroni, "In the middle of the valley, about sixty tie-cutters and graders of Young's group pitched their tents near cabins of other railroad workers," wrote Mr. Kelly. "Pine forests on the hills surrounding the valley provided material for thousands of ties, and the well-known Leroux Springs nearby furnished domestic and stock water."

These peaceful pursuits were interrupted by rumors of an impending Indian uprising. Some one hundred thirty miles to the southeast on the Fort Apache Indian Reservation the Coyotero Apaches were being whipped into a frenzy by a medicine man named Nock-ay-del-klinne. Powerful and influential, he promised to bring some of the Apache war chiefs back to life, including the fierce Diablo. Then, he told them, the Apaches would make war and drive away the white man. So serious did this become that in August 1881, the commander at Fort Apache, General E. A. Carr, with some eighty troopers and twenty-three Indian scouts went to the Apache encampment on Cibecue Creek to arrest the medicine man. The arrest had taken place, and the soldiers were going into camp, when some of the Apache scouts mutinied and joined other Indians in attacking the troopers. In the ensuing battle the medicine man and several soldiers were killed. The troops retired to the fort, and several of the treacherous scouts were executed. At about the same time, other Apaches raided the Pleasant Valley-Cherry Creek ranches west of Cibecue.

All of this caused considerable alarm at the camp on Leuroux Prairie, and Young moved to fortify a long, cabin-like structure he had already built. "To meet the expected attack," wrote Mr. Kelly, "Young and his men built a stockade fort of double-length ties in the middle of Leroux Prairie. The fort was named after Moroni, the angel who gave inscribed tablets to Joseph Smith as told in the Book of Mormon. Double ties, set on end in a shallow ditch, formed a stockade wall about twelve feet high and about one hundred feet long on each of three sides (the dwelling forming the fourth). A firing parapet, loopholes, and gates on the east and west sides completed the structure. Within the stockade, Young's men made brush and canvas shelters, and settlers in the valley congregated near the fort."

An account by Mr. Ralph Murphy, who as a boy had moved closer to the fort with his family, appeared in the same issue of

End of the long structure that was one side of the Fort Moroni stockade. Double-length railroad ties formed the other three sides. Though it was built to defend civilians against Indian attacks, it was never a military fort. (Courtesy Arizona Historical Society)

Plateau magazine, edited by Mr. Kelly. He recounted that John Young's brother had brought the alarm to his home, and had sent wagons to transport family members and their possessions to quarters nearer the fort. Concerning the fort, this article said: "The method they followed was to cut the ties double length in the woods, then haul them to the right-of-way and cut them in two there. The wagon boxes had been set off and the wagon reaches lengthened out, and the double length ties set on the bolsters of the running gears. The teamsters were instructed to bring their loads into camp, where they were stood up in the trench, close together to make solid walls. Log cabins were built aginst the wall on the inside..."

"A garrison was organized from construction crews," continued Mr. Kelly, "with two 'companies' acting as guards day and night. In addition to personal sidearms and rifles of the guard companies, Young was said to have armed the fort with an English elephant gun which fired a one-inch ball." However, the Apaches had seen their medicine man killed, had lost the battle at Cibecue Creek, and had failed in a direct attack on Fort Apache. The uprising was over, and Fort Moroni was never attacked.

The railroad reached Flagstaff on August 1, 1882, Young's contract had been carried out, and his men took up homesteads in the area. The cabin-like structure on one side of the fort was extended to a hundred feet long, on the north side. "The cabin was divided into six rooms, presumably to house Young's six wives," related Kelly. "Six doors and eight windows faced the enclosed stockade yard and a gabled split shingle roof covered the building. A powder magazine, in the west end of the cabin, had vertical log siding and a hip roof slightly higher than the rest of the roof line. Other walls of the cabin were of horizontal squared and fitted logs except for the east end which was of tall horizontal square timbers. Floor joists probably rested on large stones as no foundation appears in photographs."

John Young himself formed the Moroni Cattle Company, and used the fort as the company's headquarters. The following year, 1883, Young with several New York City businessmen as partners formed the Arizona Cattle Company out of the Moroni company. The Arizona Cattle Company was also called the "A-1" because of its brand. At one time it had some 16,000 cattle grazing a range that extended from Lake Mary on the south to the Grand Canyon on the north, and from the Little Colorado River on the east to Ash Fork on the west. "A visitor at about this time described the fort as follows: 'The settlement consists of a fort, a couple of dozen log houses, wood-choppers' shanties, commissary, etc. . . . Mr. Young's apartments are built up along one side of the stockade, inside. He has them pretty well fitted up, the floors carpeted, nice furniture, piano, and the walls hung with paintings and portraits of Brigham Young, and the Mormon saints. Fencing foils and all kinds of guns lying around, among them an inch-bore elephant gun. There was a pretty good sized library in Mr. Young's rooms, and the latest papers and magazines.' "

Young gave up his interests in the Arizona Cattle Company in 1885 and left Arizona when federal warrants were issued against him charging polygamy. The treasurer of the A-1 Cattle Company, who would become its president, was Charles L. Rickerson, and the fort was renamed Fort Rickerson in his honor. In December of that year, B. B. Bullwinkle, one time fire chief of Chicago, replaced Young as manager of the A-1 ranch. Bullwinkle, a colorful and energetic man, rounded up stray cattle, improved cattle tanks, and fenced tracts of grazing land. He also had the stockade wall (at Fort Moroni/Rickerson) cut to fence height and a large barn built. Several small outbuildings, a well, and a telephone line from Flagstaff to the fort were added during the early years of the A-1's operation.

"A long shed with double doors at one end was built against the rear wall of the cabin. The ranch and fort was described . . . as follows: 'The stockade fence surrounding the fort has been cut down to a respectable height, and the enclosure, with windmill in one corner and house on the side, has a neat, homelike appearance; more so than before when it looked grim and forbidding with his high stockade fence.' The log cabin was used for sleeping rooms, a kitchen and offices. A flag must have given the ranch headquarters an unusually official appearance," wrote Kelly.

What Bullwinkle lacked in ranching experience he made up in resolve. He also had a huge appetite for life, and was fond of beautiful women, good liquor, high stakes poker games and fast horses. He rode the seven miles to Flagstaff at a full gallop, and it was his ambition to make the distance in seven minutes. It is said that he rode more than one horse to death in the attempt. He was killed when thrown from a horse racing toward Flagstaff in May 1887. Witnesses saw him go down, and doctors were quickly brought to attend him, to no avail. His death was mourned throughout all of northern Arizona. Frank Livermore took over as the A-1 range boss.

The foundation ranges of the Arizona Cattle Company and the other huge cattle outfit in northern Arizona at the time, the Aztec Land and Cattle Company known as the famed "Hash Knife" outfit, were lands bought from the railroad company.

Fort Valley north of Flagstaff, San Francisco Peaks in the background. In this valley stood Fort Moroni, built by John Young in 1881. Later the name was changed to Fort Rickerson. There are no ruins remaining.

Since the federal government wanted to see the transcontinental railroad completed, but neither the government nor private companies had that kind of money, the government gave to the railroad companies the public lands on either side of the tracks for ten miles, checkerboarding every other section. The railroad companies thus could sell the lands and get back the money they had invested. Evidences of this checker-boarding can still be discerned today. Both the A-1 and Hashknife outfits were financed by eastern capitalists who bought huge tracts from the railroads at fifty cents per acre.

"In the early 1890s, the Arizona cattle bubble burst due to overgrazing, prolonged drought, and an economic panic of 1893," said Mr. Kelly in concluding his article. "In 1899 the Babbitt brothers of Flagstaff bought out the A-1 operations, and from 1899 to 1904, Fort Rickerson became the headquarters for the Babbitt C O Bar Ranch. The remaining posts of the stockade were removed by 1904. After that year, the Babbitt headquarters were moved to Hart Prairie and the old fort was used only occasionally during roundups. The log cabin of the fort was completely razed in 1920 by orders from a foreman of a stock tank construction crew, but without authorization from William Babbitt, manager of the C O Bar. The Babbitt brothers had wanted to retain the old fort as an historic building. No remains of the log cabin may be seen today [1964]. A few old ties and ruins of the large barn, collapsed by heavy snowfalls, mark the site of Fort Moroni."

Now not even that remains. The once-peaceful, then for a time bustling, then peaceful again valley is studded with vacation homes, and permanent dwellings as a subdivision of Flagstaff. Probably few of its residents know the rich history of the land they occupy, and even fewer of those who zip along toward the Grand Canyon or the Snow Bowl. All of the ghosts of old Fort Moroni have been laid to rest.

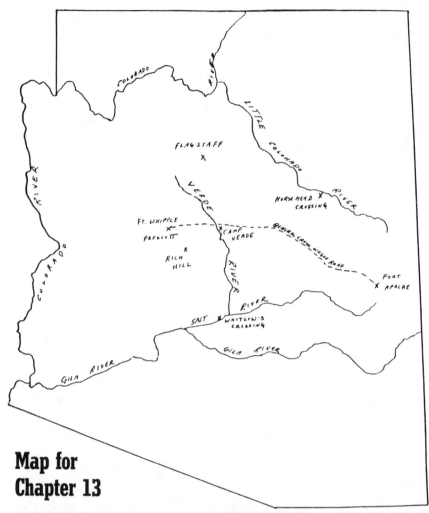

**Map for
Chapter 13**

Line of soldiers at Fort Whipple near Prescott in the 1880s.
(Courtesy Sharlot Hall Museum)

CHAPTER 13
Fort Misery, Berado's Station Whitlow's Crossing, General Crook Wagon Road

There are, of course, many spots in Arizona other than those which were subjects of chapters in this book which once were prominent, but now are obscure, for which little record of any kind can be found. There are only short references, scraps of information to be found in old manuscripts, letters and newspaper files. References to a few of these fascinating spots are recounted in this last chapter.

One was called "Fort Misery," with sardonic and pointed frontier humor, but it, like Fort Moroni, was occupied by civilians and never a military fort. There were three Fort Miserys at one time or another, two of which still exist. Fort Misery number two has even come back into prominence. It has been moved to the grounds of the Sharlot Hall Museum in Prescott and restored to probably even better condition than when it was first built. It can be visited during the museum's open hours.

The story of Fort Misery is principally to be found in the museum's research library's file of newspaper accounts, some from unidentified newspapers, but mostly from the *Arizona Miner* and the *Prescott Courier.* There are differences in the newspaper stories in some particulars. All agree that the original Fort Misery was built by a Mexican named Manuel Ysario, at the south border of Prescott, in a place called Goose Flat on Granite Creek. He arrived with wagons of goods drawn by ox teams, built a rude shelter at first, merely a log corral with two sides covered, and opened for business. Some say that Ysario was a wandering merchant who accompanied the first territorial governor, John N. Goodwin, and his party from Fort Wingate, New Mexico, and opened for business on Granite Creek on December 24th, 1863. History records, however, that the Goodwin party did not arrive in Arizona until December 27th, at Navajo Springs just across the New Mexico border, and that there the flag was raised and the territorial officials took their oaths of office on December 29th. They then traveled to Chino

Valley, where they remained until April. This difference in dates is one reason to doubt that Ysario emigrated from New Mexico, along with a letter in the museum's file which we shall presently examine.

Ysario improved his "rude shelter" into a log house, the first erected in what was to be the town of Prescott. Its location at Goose Flat was "right where Granite Street makes the elbow after crossing the bridge from the south." When his stock of goods ran out, Ysario did not replenish it but wandered on again, vacating the log house. It was taken over by a Mexican woman, one of the first women in Prescott and perhaps the most colorful of the cabin's occupants, known as Virgin Mary. She was given that nickname because of her many benevolences, and she ran a boarding house in the cabin. Her boarding price was twenty-five dollars a week in gold, which she collected in advance from the miners who patronized it. Virgin Mary had two goats, and could offer her boarders fresh milk, something rare on the frontier. When a man named Jackson opened a competing boarding house and tried to undercut Mary with a rate of sixteen dollars in gold, Mary kept her customers with her goat's milk, while the best Jackson could do was a few stewed apples along with the regular menu of venison, bread and coffee. A margin note in the file gives Mary's real name as Mrs. Cornelius Ramos. Later, she owned a ranch on Lynx Creek, where she died in 1876 and was buried in an unmarked grave.

When Virgin Mary vacated the cabin, Judge John Blinkey Howard moved in. Howard was one of the first attorneys in the territory, and one of Mary's boarders. Some accounts say that when the judge moved in he noted the leaky sod roof and named the cabin "Fort Misery," another that the justice dispensed at the cabin, and the misery of those who received it led to the cabin's name. A letter in the museum's files from a lady who as a child knew Judge Howard says that Howard himself told her the name came from the fact that he was such a poor cook, compared with Judge Fleury of the governor's house, that eating at his table was more misery than pleasure.

Judge Howard, nevertheless, upgraded the cabin into a law office and residence as well, as it was also his kitchen, parlor and bedroom. Said one account, "Inside, the walls are artistically ornamented with ancient and modern designs, and immediately over the bed is suspended a fine picture of His Holiness, Pius XI.

One of the pieces of furniture, an old chair . . . was made by the hands of Aaron Worthheimer, deceased in the year 1864. Judge Howard has many old papers and relics of the early days of this county . . ." The building also served a number of other purposes.

In the building was held the first term of court after the organization of the territory with Judge Allyn on the bench. In it the first grand jury ever held in the county deliberated. Judge Turner, then on the bench as an appointee of Abraham Lincoln, gave the jury a long and dignified charge, then the jurors retired to one end of the building and were in session for three hours. Not a single case was presented to them, and they were discharged. It is said that in it was held the first religious service in Prescott, and that the survey of the original Prescott townsite started from it, as the surveyors lived there while they laid out the town in May 1864.

During Judge Howard's occupancy it became the general headquarters for all his friends, which included everyone, and among them were some of the most famous names in the territory. "There the latch string," it was written, "hung ever on the outer wall, and the smile, as well as the liquid that cheers, always on tap," And, "(Howard's) hospitality was so broad and his modesty so profound that among his stranger guests he was the last one that would be singled out for the landlord. Everybody ran the "shack" but the owner in those days. Around his generous sideboard the heroic fathers of the territory were wont to gather, there to plan campaigns against the lurking savage, to lay plans for the weal of their beloved territory, to assist the unfortunate comrade or congratulate the successful brother on his triumph. Magnificent, patriotic, tender, noble-hearted heroes, each and every one of them . . ."

Earlier reference was made to a letter in the Sharlot Hall Museum's Library relative to whether the builder of the cabin, Manuel Ysario, actually accompanied Governor Goodwin's party into Arizona. The letter is addressed to "Tom" from the town of Quartzsite and is unsigned, but attributed to George Genung, a pioneer who lived long in the Prescott area but later moved to Quartzsite. Part of the letter, telling of a gold panning expedition in the Bradshaw mountains, reads,

"...After eating a hearty supper with Uncle Joe of bacon, beans, sourdough bread and strong coffee with sugar I went across the creek and bought a bill of grub from the Mexican whose name was Yesarea (Ysario). He afterwards built a long, three-room log building, and covered it with dirt, which was the first store built or kept in Prescott and stood right where Granite Street makes the elbow after crossing the bridge from the south. And the log house aforesaid was in later years occupied by John Howard, Atty. at law, and named by him Fort Misery. Later years, the judge becoming more prosperous changed his abode and place of business to a much more pretentious structure, one log higher and covered with split shakes. Still the name clung to the place, and it is still known as Fort Misery."

The judge indeed built a new dwelling, at a date seemingly unrecorded anywhere. A story in an unidentified newspaper in 1907 says "... When the store ceased to exist John Howard employed Sam Miller and others to haul the logs and had erected the log cabin which now stands on South Montezuma Street, and he gave that the name of 'Fort Misery,' taken from the abandoned Fort Misery to the south." A later story says he named it 'New Fort Misery,' It was this building on South Montezuma Street, number two on our list of three, that was moved to the museum grounds. The above reference to the 'abandoned Fort Misery to the south' implies that the original house built by Ysario on Granite Creek was left to eventually be consumed by the elements. This premise is reinforced by an article in the *Weekly Miner* in 1878 about a visit to Prescott by a Dr. Swetnam of Camp Verde. Concerning the visit of the doctor, who had been a member of that first grand jury meeting in the original building, the article said "... He then visited old

Judge John Howard with family and friends at "Fort Misery" on South Montezuma Street, circa 1893. (Courtesy Sharlot Hall Museum)

"Fort Misery," the little old log hut which stands under the big cottonwood trees in Goose Flat..."

Judge Howard, at the age of 71, took a bride to his 'New Fort Misery' in 1892, but in a short time they moved to a midwestern state. A gap then appears in the history of the log house. Eventually it was abandoned as a residence. The 1907 newspaper article says, "Today, the old cabin looks about the same. A sheet iron roof covers the old...roof; the street has been graded up in front so that entrance by the front door can no longer be had, as the street is graded half-way up the east wall. On the west, however, the front is the same." Neglected and almost forgotten, it was used for storage by its owners. It escaped a flood in 1891, and a big fire in 1900. It was not until the 1930s that the historic building was rescued, dismantled piece by piece, and re-assembled on the old capitol grounds where the original governor's mansion has been restored. The *Prescott Courier* of 1955 stated that the old cabin would be made over into a replica of a pioneer law office, dedicated to all lawyers in northern Arizona. It was furnished with relics of the past era such as could be found, and with old records, and law books, and stands today awaiting visitors to enjoy it as it did a hundred years ago.

We should not neglect Fort Misery number three, however. It had nothing to do with numbers one and two, except that it was given the same name. Fort Misery number three is deep in the rugged Bradshaw Mountains southeast of Prescott. It is on a four-wheel drive road that branches off the old Senator Highway that ran from Prescott to the Peck Mine. Near Crown King, at the site of the old Bradshaw City which completely disappeared years ago, the branch road leaves the highway to descend into a deep canyon, at the bottom of which are the vandalized remains of the ghost town of Oro Belle. About four more miles along this road is Fort Misery number three, and from there the road threads through the mountains past Castle Hot Springs, eventually to arrive at Lake Pleasant.

Just when the old house that is the Bradshaw Mountains' 'Fort Misery' was built seems to be unknown. Mr. Lyle Carnal, now a highly-respected real estate broker in Tempe but earlier in his life a working cowhand in Colorado and Arizona, recalls it from the times he herded cattle in the area. The *Arizona Republic* of February 17, 1972, carried an interview with Mrs. William Nelson of Glendale who was born in Oro Belle in 1906 and had some highly interesting reminiscences to recount. "The house was built by a man named Al Francis," said Mrs. Nelson. "He came to the country with a team of horses and helped build the railroad at Crown King. There never was a fort there. Francis used the 'misery' term as a figure of speech because of the hard times and the loneliness of the remote place. He later worked in the mines and ran cattle in the area and often visited friends in Crown King. Before he returned to his home, he'd remark, 'Guess I'll go back to Fort Misery.' Later owners of the property carried on the name."

Mrs. Nelson also recalled a Civil War veteran named William Bell but who was called "Old Kentuck" by his neighbors. Bell built an unusual home by Humbug Creek partially inside the hill. When Bell died at past ninety years of age, he was buried on top of the hill, where a stark, white granite marker that still remains was erected. "The tombstone arrived by train in Crown King," recalled Mrs. Nelson. "Al Francis hauled it to Fort Misery in a wagon. He and a man named Burro John set it up on the hill." There is little doubt that Fort Misery number three took its wry name from its Prescott predecessors.

Berado's Station

Another spot with fragmentary but fascinating history is intertwined with the incomplete story of an interesting but elusive man. The place was known as Berado's Station near the present town of Holbrook, and the man had several spellings of his name such as Bernardo Freyes or Freyre and Berado Frayde. A story about him in the *Arizona Miner* published in Prescott on December 29, 1876 seems to settle the fact that they are all one and the same person, a victim of often unsteady spelling on the frontier. A necessary preface to the newspaper story is recording the fact that in 1863 an adventurer named A. H. Peeples assembled in Yuma a party of like individuals to explore the Arizona interior looking for gold. Their guide was the intrepid and able scout and mountain man, Pauline Weaver, and one of the members of it was Jack Swilling, who turns up in a number of other places in Arizona history. Though sometimes called the 'Weaver party' or 'Swilling party,' it was organized by Peeples.

The Peeples expedition in addition to the principals had a retinue of employees, mostly Mexican, to handle the pack animals and do other routine camp work. In time it came to a place in central Arizona like thousands of others, rough and rocky, where a stream ran at the base of a hill, but in the creek the party panned out some gold. They named it Weaver Creek in honor of their guide. Some accounts say that the next morning some of the pack animals were found to have strayed, and the Mexican handlers ascended the hill looking for them. The Mexicans returned with their pockets full of gold nuggets they found on top of the hill, and the rush was on. The hill was sometimes called Rich Hill or Antelope Hill. So much for prefaces.

The previously mentioned newspaper story follows in its entirety.

"Bernardo Freyes, the discoverer of the rich placers on Antelope Hill in the county several years ago, and which was the cause of the first great rush of miners to this part of Arizona, is now located with his family on the Little Colorado, where he runs a station, and we are informed by those recently in from there that he still remembers the people of this section with great kindness, and frequently refuses to take a cent from those who stop with him, provided they belong to the old-timers who were here at the time he was taking out his thousands per day. He belonged to Swilling's party of five who were encamped at what is now called Weaver in 1863 when one day Freyes wandered up to the top of the hill where almost by pure accident he came upon the rich deposit of gold, lying some of it exposed to plain view on the rocks. The excitement that it produced throughout the coast and even beyond the Rocky range is still remembered by thousands who were attracted to Arizona in consequence. After partially exhausting his claim on the hill, Freyes returned to Sonora with a large amount of money, but was dissatisfied with the slow-coach way of doing things in his native land and returned to the Little Colorado in this country where he is well-fixed and takes special delight in entertaining his old friends of early days in Arizona."

As is to be expected, this account varies with others, and there is no way to reconcile them. Others say Freyes was an employee of Swilling, who filed the claims and picked up gold estimated as high as $25,000 worth. Freyes, it is said, was given $3,000 and returned to Sonora. If so, he did not stay there long, as it is also reported that he was back in Arizona in time to be in the crew that surveyed the first Prescott townsite. Another story in the *Miner* had him living in Flagstaff for a time.

Freyes next turns up at Berado's Station at the small settlement of Horsehead Crossing on the Little Colorado River. Some stories about these antecedents of the present city of

Holbrook say that the name of Horsehead Crossing came from the necessity of having horses swim the river when it was at flood stage, when all one could see was the horses' heads. Others say that the only solid-bottom crossing of the Little Colorado was at a point where the Rio Puerco joins it near Holbrook, where the meeting of these two streams caused a formation that looked like a horse's head, thus the name of the crossing.

In this location traffic naturally converged, and it is said that here in 1871 one Juan Padilla had established a trading post and stage station. In this version Padilla is said to have turned the station over to Bernardo, or Berado, to run, and the little-schooled Berado who had trouble with arithmetic simply priced everything at fifty cents for any services or goods sold. The remaining information that can be found about the station is contained in a masters thesis by Harold Wayte, a copy of which is in the library of the Arizona Historical Society. Bernardo had married a Mexican girl in New Mexico and brought her to the trading post, where, it is said, he had established a stage station, store, saloon, post office, and corral for travelers' horses, and was well established by 1876, the year of the aforementioned story in the *Arizona Miner.*

In the later 1870s, a stagecoach passenger noticed a girl with golden hair and blue eyes waiting on tables. This was not in keeping with the darker complexion of Bernardo and his wife, who called the girl "Crismus," arousing the curiosity of the passenger enough for him to inquire of Bernardo why he called her that. Several years earlier on a Christmas Day, related Bernardo, a buckboard had been found standing beside a road near Leroux Wash. The nearly naked dead bodies of a man and woman lay beside a cold campfire, the horses had been killed, the camp looted, and everything the murderers could not use they had thrown into the campfire.

The driver of the stagecoach that came upon the tragic scene spotted a large piece of canvas a short distance away. Upon lifting one corner he found a little girl, possibly three years old. sound asleep from exhaustion. She could tell the driver nothing about what had happened, or about the murdered couple. The driver took her to Bernardo, who took her into his home and raised her as one of his own.

The murders were partially solved a few days after they occurred when two men, well-mounted and leading a heavily-

Part of the original General Crook Trail, now designated as FS 300, winds through the Coconino National Forest above the Mogollon Rim.

laden pack mule, rode into Berado's station. That night they got drunk, picked a fight with the bartender whom they shot in the shoulder, but who then killed them both. In their packs was evidence that they were the murderers of the couple found at Leroux Wash. After holding the mens' horses and supplies for a year, the sheriff sold them and gave the money, with that taken from the dead men, to Bernardo, who had become the child's legal guardian. Bernardo put the money in the bank at Albuquerque to hold for the little girl.

By 1881, the Atlantic and Pacific railroad company was laying tracks only two miles from Horsehead Crossing, and its railroad camp evolved into the town of Holbrook. Inevitably, the settlement at Horsehead Crossing and Berado's station were doomed. One version is that Berado closed up and moved to Albuquerque. Wayte's version is a sadder one. There was a distant neighbor, Harold Huning, partner with Colonel Corydon Cooley in a large ranch where the town of Show Low later sprang up. As a land owner and cattleman and owner of a large store, Huning was wealthy and influential. Some say that Huning stole Bernardo's wife, others that she simply left Bernardo for Huning. In any event, she took her children and went to live with Huning. Bernardo left the territory and was lost to history.

Whitlow's Crossing

There were other river crossings where little settlements that sprang up because of them, and became prominent in early Arizona, later disappeared. Another such was Whitlow's Crossing of the Salt River north of the then farming community of Lehi near Mesa. On the north side of the Salt River at the crossing was a little settlement where Charles Whitlow lived for a time. One William Rowe followed him shortly and established a stage stop known as Rowe's Station. The original company of those Mormon colonizers who found the communty at Lehi, and later the city of Mesa, crossed the Salt River here in 1877.

Whitlow had arrived in 1865 coincident with the establishment of Fort McDowell on the Verde River a few miles to the north. He was a supplier of hay for the animals at the fort, and kept a general store. Rowe moved with his family to the crossing and built a station there in 1868. The location became important because it was at the river crossing of Fort McDowell's main supply road from its terminus at Maricopa Wells to the south, and at the intersection of this road with the stagecoach trail from Phoenix. This proximity to Fort McDowell did not deter the Apache Indians, who regularly raided the settlers' corrals and drove off their draft animals and cows. The cows' milk was badly needed to feed the families, and the settlers were always in need from loss of their animals and the rigors of frontier life.

Whitlow's Crossing, which Whitlow tried to re-name "Maryville" for his twelve-year-old daughter, despite its struggles had its good moments and at times gave a good imitation of other Western towns. It organized the Maryville Irrigating Canal Company and had a ditch flowing with 10,000 miners inches. It had a store, hotel, blacksmith and carpentry shops and envisioned a business district. There was a school taught by Dr. T. J. Wilson, but Wilson had been there only a short time when he was robbed by one Thomas Maxwell. Maxwell was pursued by Rowe and his son, who severely wounded the robber and brought him back to the settlement where he died. There was even a gun battle on February 1, 1873, between James Beatty and Richard McGregor, in which Beatty was killed. A post office was established in April 1873, with Whitlow as postmaster, but it was discontinued the following January.

Whitlow's Crossing began to decline with the opening of others more convenient, particularly Hayden's Ferry, and the gradual phase-out and eventual closing of Fort McDowell sealed its fate. The settlers moved away, Whitlow and his family to the Florence area, where he became a prominent cattleman. His name was given to Whitlow Dam east of Mesa, which impounds the waters of Queen Creek in the Superstition foothills. Whitlow himself is buried in the old Adamsville cemetery, to which reference is made in another chapter of this book.

General Crook Wagon Road

The last of our once-prominent but now obscure places is another that has in recent times experienced a partial resurrection. It was called the General Crook Wagon Road, built at the command of the general from Fort Whipple near Prescott to Fort Verde in the Verde River valley, and on over the mountains to Fort Apache on the then newly-established Apache Indian Reservation. Portions of it have recently been remarked by the U.S. Forest Service as the General Crook Trail for hikers and horseback trail riders.

General George Crook was assigned as commander of the military district of Arizona early in 1871, and arrived soon afterward at Fort Whipple, the district's headquarters. His experience as an Indian fighter on the plains had convinced him that well-mounted and well-supplied units, able to move quickly and attack in surprise, were vital in Indian campaigns. He also found it necessary to recruit Indians loyal to the U.S. government as scouts to trail the renegade bands and fight alongside the troops. His first inspection of his Arizona facilities told him that Forts Verde and Apache, isolated in the virgin wilderness in the heart of Apache country, must be connected to their main supply base at Fort Whipple with a good road, so that troops and supplies could be moved in a hurry.

The general himself with a detachment of his troops made the first reconnaisance of the layout of the road, moving westward from Fort Apache late in 1871. Early in 1872 a pack trail was being routed and marked eastward from Fort Whipple; in 1873 pack trains began moving along it. In 1874 the first wagon trains began rolling over the road. In general the road took routes from Prescott now followed by the Cherry Creek Road, down Copper Canyon near what is now Interstate 17 to the Verde Valley and Camp Verde, northeastward ascending the Mogollon Rim to skirt the deep Fossil Creek Canyon, along the edge of the great Mogollon Rim eastward to Cooley's Ranch where the town of Show Low would spring up, thence southeasterly to Fort Apache.

This was no small undertaking. The some-two hundred miles of road had to be hewn out of the trackless wilderness with manpower and horse and mule power. There was no power equipment; there were axes, mauls and shovels, there were drags for leveling, and chains and ropes for pulling stumps and moving rocks. There was no cut-and-fill or culverts laid in stream beds and a road built over them. It was down the side of an arroyo, crossing the stream bed at its bottom, and up the other side. It meant skirting boggy morasses and rocky pinnacles, and cutting a path through dense forests. Each mile was marked, in open country with a boulder that had the mileage carved into it; in forested country the trees were blazed or carved with the mileage. Some of these markers, boulders and ancient pines and oaks, are still to be found today.

The General Crook Wagon Road has more recently been remembered for its stretch between Fort Verde and Fort Apache, and for the scenic portion along the top edge of the Mogollon Rim. From Fort Verde its route swung north over the rim, and today a paved road designated as a forest highway, FH 9, closely parallels it or in some places drives right over the old road bed. Half-way up the rim is a prominent landmark named Rock Butte, at the foot of which on the highway is a historical marker. At this marker is the original thirteen-mile marker, a boulder with the carving on it. Some twenty miles farther, up the rim and across the plateau, the paved FH 9 joins Arizona State Route 87.

A few miles north along Highway 89 is a junction with the Old Rim Road going east, which is the approximate route of the General Crook Wagon Road. The Old Rim Road is designated Forest Service Route 300, and follows closely, sometimes in the same road bed, the General Crook Wagon Road. The rim road cuts across Milk Ranch Point, passing Baker Butte, said to have been named for an army surgeon named Baeker. On the butte is a fire control tower, from the top of which on a clear day most of central Arizona can be seen, from the high mesas of the Hopi Indian Reservation on the north to the Santa Catalina Mountains near Tucson to the south.

Soon the road comes out on the edge of the Mogollon Rim,

affording breath-taking views of the valleys and farther-away mountain ranges to the south. Again, the Old Rim Road follows closely the General Crook Wagon Road along the rim, sometimes in the same road bed. Other roads lead off to the rim lakes; one goes to the site of the Battle of Big Dry Wash fought between Apaches and troops, where a metal plate attached to a larger boulder serves as a battle monument. The rim road passes a cabin where it is said that General Crook himself rested from his travels along the road but was actually built about 1900. Beyond the rim, the General Crook Wagon Road followed the approximate route of Arizona State Highway 260 to the point where the Old Rim Road, Forest Service Route 300, leaves it to the east. Again the wagon road followed the route of the Old Rim Road for another fifteen miles. Then it followed a route between the rim road and the highway into Showlow. From there it closely followed the boundary fence of the Fort Apache Indian Reservation to Hon-dah and along the present highway to Fort Apache.

For many years after the last Apache bands had moved to the reservation, the General Crook Wagon Road was used by troops on patrol, and by civilian traffic. The Old Rim Road was built in 1928, and by this time there were other, more direct roads to destinations along the wagon road's route. Since it was no longer needed as a military route, the wagon road fell into disuse. Some of it was incorporated into roads later built, and some portions of it though not part of the road system can still be discerned and traveled today.

So we reach the end of our journey to Arizona's historic places now fallen into obscurity. To actually visit them, to stand where the valiant pioneers stood, where the men and women who fill our historical records lived the lives and the deeds recorded for us, whether noble or base, is an exercise in awe and wonder. We think of them as the innocents of an outmoded world, and of ourselves as the sophisticates of a modern civilization. None of us will be here in another century of time, to judge whether in the past hundred years the tide of civilization they pushed forward, then passed on to us, has advanced or retreated.

Bibliography

Ahnert, Gerald. *Retracing the Butterfield Overland Trail Through Arizona.* Los Angeles: Westernlore Press, 1973.

Altshuler, Constance Wynn. *Latest from Arizona: The Hesperian Letters, 1859-1861.* Tucson: Arizona Historical Society, 1969.

Axford, Joseph. *Around Western Campfires.* Tucson: University of Arizona Press, 1969.

Barnes, Will C. *Arizona Place Names.* Ed. Byrd Granger. Tucson: University of Arizona Press, 1960.

Bolton, Herbert. *Anza's California Expedition, Vol. 1.* New York: Russell & Russell, 1966.

Bolton, Herbert. *Kino's Historical Memoirs of Pimeria Alta.* Berkeley: University of California Press, 1948.

Bond, Ervin. *Cochise County, Past & Present.* Douglas, AZ: privately published, 1982.

Bowman, Eldon. *A Guide To The General Crook Trail.* Flagstaff: Museum of Northern Arizona Press, 1978.

Breakenridge, William. *Helldorado.* Boston: Houghton-Mifflin, 1928.

Burns, Walter N. *Tombstone; An Iliad of the Southwest.* Garden City, NY: Doubleday, 1929.

Conkling, Roscoe & Margaret. *The Butterfield Overland Mail.* Glendale, CA: The Arthur H. Clark Co., 1947.

Egan, Ferol. *The El Dorado Trail.* New York: McGraw-Hill, 1970.

Falk, Odie B. *Arizona: A Short History.* Norman: University of Oklahoma Press, 1970.

Farish, Thomas. *History of Arizona.* Phoenix: Flimer Bros., 1915.

Forbes, Robert. *Crabb's Filibustering Expedition into Sonora, 1857.* Tucson: Arizona Silhouettes, 1954.

Goff, John. *King S. Woolsey.* Cave Creek, AZ: Black Mountain Press, 1981.

Hinton, Richard. *Handbook to Arizona.* San Francisco: Payot-Upham & Co., 1878.

Lease, Paul V. *Pimas, Dead Padres, and Gold.* Menlo Park, CA: Archivists Press, 1965.

Manje, Juan Mateo. *Unknown Arizona and Sonora, 1693-1721.* Tr. Harry Karns. Tucson: Arizona Silhouettes, 1954.

Merrill, W. Earl. *One Hundred Steps Down Mesa's Past.* Mesa: privately published, 1970.

Merrill, W. Earl. *One Hundred Yesterdays.* Mesa: privately published, 1972.

Miller, Joseph. *Arizona, The Last Frontier.* New York: Hastings House, 1956.

Parsons, George W. *The Private Journal of George Whitwell Parsons.* Tombstone: Tombstone Epitaph, 1972.

Stratton, Emerson O. *Pioneering in Arizona: The Reminiscences of Emerson Oliver Stratton.* Ed. John A. Carroll. Tucson: Arizona Historical Society, 1964.

Utley, Robert. *A Clash of Cultures.* Washington, DC: National Park Service, 1977.

Willson, Roscoe. *No Place For Angels.* Tucson: Arizona Silhouettes, 1948.

Index

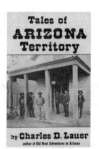

ORDER BLANK

GOLDEN WEST PUBLISHERS

☼ 4113 N. Longview Ave. • Phoenix, AZ 85014

602-265-4392 • **1-800-658-5830** • FAX 602-279-6901

Qty	Title	Price	Amount
	Arizona Adventure	6.95	
	Arizona Cook Book	5.95	
	Arizona Legends and Lore	6.95	
	Arizona Territory Cook Book	6.95	
	Arizona Trivia	8.95	
	Arizona Walls	14.95	
	Arizoniana	8.95	
	Cowboy Cartoon Cook Book	5.95	
	Cowboy Slang	5.95	
	Discover Arizona!	6.95	
	Explore Arizona!	6.95	
	Ghost Towns in Arizona	6.95	
	Hiking Arizona	6.95	
	Horse Trails in Arizona	12.95	
	In Old Arizona	6.95	
	Old West Adventures in Arizona	6.95	
	Prehistoric Arizona	5.00	
	Quest for the Dutchman's Gold	6.95	
	Tales of Arizona Territory	6.95	
	Wild West Characters	6.95	

Shipping & Handling Add ⇒	U.S. & Canada	$3.00	
	Other countries	$5.00	

☐ My Check or Money Order Enclosed $

☐ MasterCard ☐ VISA ($20 credit card minimum)

(Payable in U.S. funds)

Acct. No.   Exp. Date

Signature

Name   Telephone

Address

City/State/Zip

11/98   **Call for FREE catalog**   Old West Adventures

This order blank may be photo-copied.